BLUEPRINT
FOR
Abundance

A Self-Help and Self-Love Guide to
Abundance from the Inside Out

VONNIE VIRGIL

Business Address:
P.O. Box 59671
Chicago, IL 60659

Copy Editor: Devon Freeny
Book Design: C.B. Telemann | cbtelemann.com
Set in Scala, Scala Sans, and Poetica

ISBN 978-1-7330245-0-1

Contents

Acknowledgments

Writing your first book can be a depleting and fulfilling experience simultaneously, which is why having people to help you is of utmost importance. I've been blessed to have found professionals who were not only knowledgeable, but also willing to share their stories, time and knowledge with me for this book.

The most helpful in this endeavor was Josh Siegal, a neighbor and mentor who gave his time and information to me like a friend would. He helped lay out the entire process of publishing a book from start to finish. Several of his publishing team members have now become my team members, to include Devon Freeny and C.B. Telemann.

Also, on this list are my Trusted Readers: the handful of people who took the time to read the book in its early stages and offer priceless feedback. A very big "Thank you!" goes to Nikki Blak, Larone Ellison, Crystal Malone and Skye Frank.

Everyone Could Use a Blueprint for Financial Success!

You can have an abundance of money in life and it doesn't have to wear you out to get it. Most important, your journey to abundance can even be one of the most fulfilling journeys of your life!

Blueprint for Abundance is a handbook for anyone who is ready to experience more rewarding results from carefully managing his or her personal finances. Written by aspiring financial and life coach Vonnie Virgil, it is a refreshingly introspective guide to the process of generating and maintaining wealth. Offering a unique combination of self-help strategies, spiritual wisdom, and financial tips, Vonnie delivers advice that is at once relatable, accessible, and easy to put into practice right away.

Vonnie is not just providing the ABCs and 123s of building wealth but is also encouraging readers to pursue deeper soul work, showing them the path to abundance not only in financial matters but in every aspect of their lives. By following Vonnie's advice, you'll discover how your attitude toward money can advance or delay your financial abundance. You'll learn how to identify strategies to remove financial barriers. You'll find out how to improve the financial skills you're already good at using.

Blueprint for Abundance is an important resource that can lead you to the financial success you've always dreamed of.

CHAPTER 1

Getting Started:
The Energy of Abundance

You've done everything you've been taught to do: save, budget, and invest with your money. You've played by all the financial rules, but you have not been able to enjoy the abundance you want. Why is that? Why haven't your actions yielded more abundant results? The answer: because you need to combine the *energy of abundance* with the financial guidelines you've learned. The energy of abundance is a cool, calm, and collected attitude toward money that creates the kind of internal environment money is attracted to. When saving, budgeting, and investing alone can no longer increase your wealth, the energy of abundance is here to help you break through to the next level.

All of the financial actions you've been taking to build wealth are absolutely right and necessary. In chapter 5, we'll even run through some you may have missed. But first, we will dive into the *internal* work that's just as necessary to propel your financial life to the next level. You've learned how to "walk" financially—now let's run! Saving, budgeting, and investing are the ABCs of finances, the basic ingredients of abundance. But now that you're ready to go higher, we need to add some new ingredients to the recipe.

You Don't Need to Be an Expert

You don't need to be an expert on financial matters to generate abundance. Just like you don't have to be an expert in fitness to enjoy the benefits of working out, or an expert in writing to enjoy a good book, you don't have to be an expert in finance to produce more money. This book is for the average hardworking person who wonders why his or her prudent actions have not produced better financial results, and who is ready to follow a blueprint that has helped me generate and maintain financial abundance.

For me, nothing has been easier than making money—or, more accurately, receiving it in abundance. Not from any person or any entity—I've never been given an inheritance or won the lottery. I certainly wouldn't complain if I had, but that's not where my abundance came from. It was summoned by my energy—by who I am on the inside and by what I do on the outside. Who you are internally and what you do externally is all the power you need to enjoy more financial success. *Blueprint for Abundance* will show you how to align your internal energy with your external actions and attract all the prosperity you need.

The reason you're eager for more is because your soul is calling you to a higher level. You've probably mastered all the financial skills you've learned up to this point, and you've seen how wonderfully they can work. You may have seen how money can multiply overnight when you invest properly. Maybe you've noticed that by saving little by little you can end up with a good nest egg in less time than you predicted. You've probably discovered that when you give generously, the universe tends to speedily meet your own needs as they arise.

All of that is really magical, but I'd bet your soul still isn't quite satisfied. If you're anything like me, you've gotten to a point in life when tiny drops of financial success are no longer enough. Let's face it: You have a legacy to build. You have a family you want to give the good life. You have a destiny you're ready to fulfill—and I intend to share with you the tools, stories, and practices I've used so that you can empower your own journey to abundance.

This book will show you how to align your energy with your actions.

The Peaceful Pattern

Ever since I was a little girl growing up in Chicago, I've had a liberty in my relationship with money. If I saw a homeless person on my way to school, I sympathetically gave that person my lunch money—I was more emotionally affected by someone else's need than I was by the possibility of not having enough money to buy my own food. I learned not to worry about lunch, because somehow the universe always fed me.

Although I grew up poor, I was never afraid of not having enough money. I wasn't emotionally affected by its absence. As I became an adult and began to receive money more abundantly, I never experienced a false sense of security from its presence. Basically, I didn't feel emotional highs or lows about money. I didn't know why, because it seemed like everyone around me was freaking out about their finances for one reason or another. I guess it was an energy I was born with, and over the years, I've learned to refine that energy to my advantage. I learned that the more my attitude toward money remained restful, the more money would flow to me in abundance.

Even without the big highs and lows, maintaining a state of restfulness still took some work. When financial needs would arise, my first reaction would be to get nervous and stressed. But when I let go of the fear and just relaxed about my needs, they always seemed to be met in an unexpected way—a gift from a friend, a discount in a store, a promotion at work, or some other stroke of good fortune—and always at the perfect time, without me burning myself out to meet them.

This happened so regularly that I began to feel excited when financial needs cropped up. I began to watch for opportunities to practice managing my energy about money, because I wanted to see if it was actually a universal law that my needs would be met if I remained peaceful rather than panicked. I termed this practice the *peaceful pattern*, and I made it an easy process: when a need arose, I would 1) calm myself down and 2) continue my regular external actions regarding money. *External actions* are the routine outward practices we do with our money, like saving, budgeting, and investing.

Usually, when we humans encounter financial needs, we panic and change our external actions, tightening our grip on whatever money we have left. Our usual response is to stop saving, blow the budget, or sell our investments. But I wanted to do the opposite. While I waited on life to meet my needs, I continued to save, budget, and share with other people who had urgent needs. It was a challenge to myself to see how emotionally free I could remain in the face of my own financial difficulties. I developed an expectation that my peacefulness would somehow be rewarded.

The experiment worked: By not allowing my energy to freak out, I produced an environment in which abundance felt at home with me. My needs were always met, and there was always an abundance left over. It was like a wink from the universe rewarding me for the internal and external work.

Minor Need—Major Abundance

There have been many times the universe has met needs of mine when I intentionally practiced the peaceful pattern. Here's a true story of such a time. I once had a relatively minor need—for a new cell phone, because my old one had broken. This story took place five years ago, so needing a new cell phone was not as much of an emergency as it is today.

It was wintertime, almost Christmas day, and every store I visited was sold out of all the reasonably priced phones. I made my way to a certain cell phone service provider and was greeted by a salesperson who extended me the offer of the phone I wanted—but for a $200 cash deposit. I understood that cash deposits were occasionally required for customers who had lower credit ratings, but I had a high credit rating, so I didn't understand why a deposit was needed. Besides, it was Christmastime, and I didn't want to drop $200 of my Christmas cash when I shouldn't have had to. After about twenty minutes of double-talk, the salesperson slipped up and revealed that no deposit was really required—this was just his attempt to get me to spend cash in the store, which would result in a commission for him. I angrily left without a new cell phone, not very confident that I would be able to get one soon without spending a fortune for it.

As soon as I noticed myself fuming over this, I remembered the peaceful pattern. I decided to let go of the anger and just proceed through my day as calmly as possible. There was no point in losing the Christmas spirit over something so minor. Later that day, I was running some errands at a nearby Target store. I noticed they had a tiny cell phone section, so I decided to inquire, without much confidence I would find what I needed. The bubbly salesperson explained that not only did she have the exact phone I was looking for, but there just so happened to be a sale they had never offered before: for each phone you purchase, you also get a $200 gift card!

Not only was I not required to pay a $200 cash deposit, but I was getting $200 cash back—the exact amount the previous store attempted to take from me! I was amazed at how quickly and precisely the universe met this seemingly trivial need. It was confirmation that God had my back, rewarding me for remaining peaceful.

Money Responds to Energy
Just like everything else, money responds to energy.

Money is a part of the currency system humans have built into our existence. Most cultures need some form of currency to manage the limited resources on Earth. We all need food, water, and shelter, but these resources are perceived to be scarce. In response to that, we've created systems of currency to more easily determine who can have access to these resources in abundance. Because of this perceived scarcity, humans have invested great amounts of vital energy, both anxious and joyous, into their currency systems. This is happening all over the world all the time.

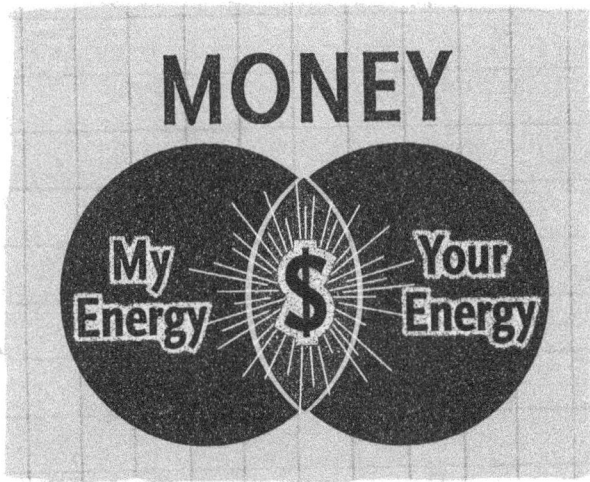

The collective energy that we have directed toward money causes it to respond to that energy. This is true about money in the same way it is true about love, health, and all the other universal needs and desires that humans have.

Anxiety specialist Sheryl Paul explains in her article

"Health Anxiety, Money Anxiety and the Fear of Loss" that
people are employing their natural survival instincts in
response to money, health, and love. As a result, we experience strong fears about money, health, and love in the
same way our ancestors experienced fears about raid-
ers threatening their physical safety. Although we don't
have as much of a need for that primal survival instinct,
Paul says, it still manifests itself in our modern thinking with questions like "Am I with the right partner? (Is
love safe?); Will I harm someone? (Am I safe?); Will I
have enough money? (Am I secure?) Do I have a termi-
nal illness? (Is life safe?) Is the planet going to be okay?
(Are we all safe?)." Almost every concern we have is now
being assigned a life-or-death kind of energy.

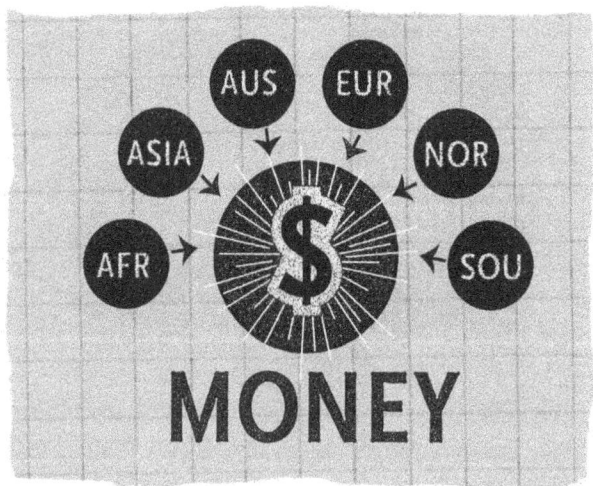

What we have forgotten is that the energy is more
powerful than the entity. Money is not energy. Money is
powerless. It's paper. In and of itself, it is no more valuable

than a sheet of paper. But money is an entity that we have assigned an enormous amount of energy to—and it is our energy that infuses it with power. Think about other entities that we infuse with power. A church is no more than a building until you put the energy of the people inside of it. Only then will it become meaningful and powerful. It is the energy that gives power to the entity.

Money will respond to the energy you assign to it—but it will respond differently depending on whether you project an energy of abundance or an energy of fear. It will respond to peaceful energy by moving toward you, and to fearful energy by moving away from you. For example, the saying "More money, more problems" has a very negative energy assigned to it. When you subscribe to this saying, you are linking money and problems together for yourself, and it will manifest that way! How about we say, "More money, more peace"? Or "More money, more opportunities to grow, to help, or to make a difference"?

Your energy makes a difference in matters of money just as it does in your personal relationships. If you've met someone you're interested in dating and you're so afraid of losing him or her that you never want that person to leave your sight, you're more likely to push the person away than to entice him or her to stay. Many of us have learned that if you want someone to feel comfortable with you, you need to have a welcoming yet liberating energy toward them that says, "I'm delighted to have you around, but you are free to come and go as you please." That is a healthier attitude toward relationships, and your relationship with money is no different.

People with a fearful attitude toward money are afraid

they'll never have enough of it, and when they do get it, they're afraid of losing it! Fear whether it comes or whether it goes. That's not healthy. A relaxed approach toward anything in life is much more likely to produce more of what you want. A tight grip on anything in life is likely to produce less of it. What we want to do is produce the best energy to attract more abundance—to be less fearful about money and more confident that the universe is at work to help us and all we need to do is tap into that.

The following chapters will show you how to do this, first in chapter 2 by defining abundance and illustrating why we can and should expect to have more of it. Chapters 3 and 4 present my blueprint for the internal practices I've used to attract more abundance in my life. And chapter 5 shares the financial advice that has helped me and others build abundance over the years. It is important that you combine the guidance in all these chapters to get the most out of your journey toward abundance. Using the financial advice alone will improve your finances, but only by combining those external actions with the internal practices can you generate the abundant financial life you desire.

It is the energy that gives power to the entity.

CHAPTER 2

What Is Abundance?

Your bills are paid. Your savings account is growing. Your retirement account is finally showing some potential. On top of all that, you can even occasionally help a friend with a loan or financial gift. You can afford to give tithes to your church. You can stray away from your budget from time to time and buy some gifts for yourself. Life ain't bad. What you have now is good—but you want great. You really want abundance.

But what *is* abundance? You might think of it as *a profusion of something, an ample amount, usually in reference to wealth.* I like this definition, but I want to give it more personal power: in the words of bestselling self-help author Wayne Dyer, "*Abundance is not something we acquire. It's something we tune into.*" Abundance is that space inside of you that holds everything you need to be completely fulfilled.

If you tune into that space—sit there and eavesdrop on it—you will hear million-dollar ideas: songs, books, artwork, websites, businesses. You will hear your destiny speaking to you. The power to get wealth is brewing inside of you just waiting to be realized. If I were to combine the more common definition with Dyer's definition, I would say that abundance is *a profusion of power and energy that we can tune into to attain an ample amount of all that we need.*

Why Do We Need Abundance?

What's wrong with just being content with what we already have? There is nothing wrong with it—unless you want something else. If we are truly happy with what we have, there is no need to venture out for more. But if you want more than what you already have, your energy is going to start enforcing that. In one way or another, you are going to start attracting what you really want and need. You are going to start taking actions, maybe even unconsciously, to obtain it.

If you are ready for abundance to the point that you would take the necessary steps to obtain it, then abundance is a *need* for you now. If you're not ready, then you don't need it yet and you don't have to reach for it yet. It's like a baby learning to walk. It's perfectly okay if a baby doesn't know how to walk yet. That's suitable for the level of life the baby is on. But when she is ready to walk to the point that she begins to take her first steps, then walking has become a need for her—and she will walk by any means necessary. If you've ever witnessed a toddler learning to walk, you know they are relentless. They will fall a hundred times and bounce right back up for another round. For the baby who is ready to walk, nothing can keep it from walking. It is the same for *you*. That's why *you* need abundance—because you want it; you're ready for it. It has been aroused in you. And now that you desire it, it desires you too.

"Abundance is not something we acquire. It's something we tune into." – Wayne Dyer

Aggressive Abundance

When you develop a need for more, your energy will begin to set things in motion toward that. All of your combined actions will signal to the universe it is time to bestow what your soul is calling forth. I know the story of a woman who experienced this. She had become wildly successful in her media career, but she wanted to be an actress. She had already achieved great success as a journalist, public figure, and motivational speaker. She was even a household name in her field. But she became obsessed with getting a certain acting role, and she couldn't put it out of her mind. Now, most people might say, "Hey, lady, you've got it all already—the money and prestige. You should be happy where you are. Why do you want to be an actress? What if you go into acting and fail?"

I'm sure all those thoughts ran through that woman's mind—she probably even had people say things like that to her face. But this woman already had the hope in her soul. She wasn't after any more money or prestige. She had an abundance of that already. But her soul wanted abundance in the field of acting. She probably felt that she should just be content with where she was, and in the face of all the doubt, she may have tried to pray the desire away. But even if she tried to mentally abandon the desire, it had already taken root in her soul, and in the universe.

Without even trying, she began to show up at the right places at the right times, to be seen by the right people. Filmmakers and casting directors had been watching her and she didn't even know it.

Because of her desire, she attracted one of the most classic movie roles: Sofia in Steven Spielberg's *The Color Purple*. Yes, I'm talking about Ms. Oprah Winfrey. She even said herself, "I had drawn *The Color Purple* into my life" without knowing the who's who and what's what of acting.

As I said, there is nothing wrong with being content with what you have, but if your soul wants more, it will create more. It will attract more. Abundance has less to do with what you already have and more to do with who you are and what you want. You don't have to be poor to want more. You can be wherever you are in life, and if your soul is big, your abundance will be big too.

Look at the Birds

Our goal is to receive abundance in life without exerting painstaking effort. If you've ever watched a master at work, he or she is usually doing it effortlessly, in a state of relative restfulness and joy. I say "relative" because a UFC fighter's level of rest during a fight is different from a writer's level of rest while typing. My point is that both professionals can succeed at doing their work without wearing themselves out. Our journey to mastering abundance will be no different.

The first step toward abundance is to *relax*. I know relaxing is always easier said than done, so this may feel like condescending advice. "Chill out" is usually the last thing you want to hear when you're trying to achieve something important. Let me explain: I want you to be able to relax by knowing *why* you can relax. You will achieve mastery in abundance by relaxing—just as the birds do:

"*Look at the birds of the air; they do not sow or reap or store away in barns, and yet your heavenly Father feeds them. Are you not much more valuable than they?*"

Matthew 6:26 is one of the most well-known teachings of Jesus in the Bible. The quote explains why we can expect to be cared for in the world. In my early-adulthood days of learning to master my finances, I felt that if I could really believe this teaching then I would have less fear about having my needs met in life . . . so I decided to watch some birds.

Outside of my window, I saw a group of birds gather around a puddle of water that formed in my backyard after a rainy night. They happily drank from the puddle and even bathed in it. After a cool drink and a bath, they sauntered off and began to peck at the ground. I couldn't see what it was they were pecking at, but it was edible, and it was there in abundance. They were receiving this mysterious food effortlessly. For some reason I had the feeling that, as a human being, I was eligible for the same effortless care from the universe. In the face of doubt, I needed validation for this feeling before I could accept it, so I methodically revisited what Jesus said:

"*Look at the birds of the air*..." Step one is to stop, breathe, and relax into the moment. Bird-watching is a relaxing event.

"*They do not sow or reap or store away in barns*..." They don't do any of the external actions we do in pursuit of abundance, like invest, save and budget.

"*Yet* [in spite of not doing those external actions], *your heavenly Father* [God, the universe] *feeds them*..." Why is that? Why are they provided for in abundance like this? The answer blew me away:

"*Are you not much more valuable than they*?" Value! The answer is value! The universe provides for the birds because they have value. Even more amazing was the realization that *we* are "much more valuable"! The universe provides for us because we are valuable too.

We have value to the universe, and if we become fully conscious of that fact, we can enjoy more abundance. We must consider ourselves worthy of receiving it—not in a high-and-mighty kind of way, but with a confident awareness of who we are. My four-year-old son knows that simply because he is my son, I will feed him. He is not even conscious of this dynamic, because it has come so naturally to our relationship. Most times, my care for him is so attentive that I have food prepared for him before he even realizes he is hungry. His value to me as a *son* automatically entitles him to my loving and attentive care.

This is the same value the birds have to the universe, and it's the same value you and I have to the universe. The birds are not even conscious of their value to the universe and they are still provided for. Now I ask Jesus's question again: "Are you not much more valuable than they?" Why are we so valuable? Because we are daughters and sons of the universe. Your value as a daughter or a son automatically makes you eligible for the care and abundance you need to thrive. So, then, there are two lines of thought we need to accept: 1) we can be safe and cared for in the world, 2) because we are valuable.

Money Is a Servant

Knowing that you are valuable should not make you arrogant, but it should make you feel confident and restful. This restful energy will attract all that you need in life, including money. Money is a servant to the universe, and just as the universe uses seeds and rain puddles to serve the birds, it also uses money (among many other things) to serve us. Money should not be loved and served but be used to love and to serve, and it is of service to us because we've created the need for it. We have built the need for money into our universal existence. And now that we need it, the universe will use it to serve us.

You don't have to chase down your servant. All you need to do is beckon him. You simply request his presence and he will report for duty. But if you mistakenly believe that *you* are the servant, then your relationship with money will be distorted. You will do the serving, while money does the beckoning, and that is not the right relationship to have. Remember, you are the human here. Money was created to be in service to you—not the other way around.

The best way to avoid that warped relationship is to know and honor your value. You are not simply valuable, but *much more valuable*! This is an important ingredient in any relationship. If you enter a romantic relationship undervaluing yourself, you are not going to get the respect, honor, and care you need and deserve. But if you enter a relationship conscious of your value, you will attract respect, honor, and care in abundance. Therefore, relax in the belief that you are valuable and cared for, and approach your relationship with money with the realization that it is a servant, and it is ready to serve you.

Run Baby, Run!: Don't Chase Money

There have been times in my own experience when I misjudged my relationship with money. I would encounter a need, then get busy working. I put on my servants' clothes, tied my hair back, rolled up my sleeves, and started chasing money. I came up with plans and strategies for how to get what I needed. I took on more work, allowed myself less time to rest, and gave up precious time with my son to get the needs met. Consequently, I would make some extra money, but something odd seemed to happen. Almost every time I entered one of those frenzied money-chasing cycles, whatever extra I was able to earn would go up in smoke! New needs would pop up to consume what I'd earned, and poof! There went the money I had been chasing down.

Have you ever noticed what happens when you start chasing someone? Whoever you're chasing usually runs away! If you have a kid, start chasing him or her right now and watch what happens. That is what I was observing: the more I chased money, the more it would run away from me. My only recourse was to reenter the peaceful pattern and establish a less dependent relationship with money. To do this, I had to remind myself of the distinctions between what I do, what I have, and who I am.

Being vs. Doing vs. Having

One of my favorite spiritual teachers is Iyanla Vanzant. Her masterful mix of psychology and spirituality is mesmerizing to me. During one of her healing sessions with a client who was dealing with marital discord, she introduced the concept of being, doing, and having. Although she used this concept in the context of marriage, I will apply it to our dealings with money.

Being

Understanding your value involves understanding your *being*: not what you do or what you have, but *who you are*. And who you are is all about love. I can guarantee that when you discover who you are, you will fall in love with yourself—and there is nothing more attractive than love. Everything gravitates toward love. Money moves toward love. Love moves toward love. Business opportunities even move in the direction of love. Love is the most powerful magnet in the universe.

When you get to know and love your *being*, you will begin to draw all that you need. Are you generous? Are you honorable? Remain that way inwardly, toward yourself first, then toward others in your thoughts, and watch as generosity and honor hunt you down. But you must first identify who you are so you can align your actions with more purposeful intention.

When I identified my own *being*, I aligned my internal energy and my external actions with that. I did not want to hunt down money, because I am not a hunter. I am a stewardess. I have identified my *being* as a stewardess. Some synonyms for *stewardess* are *keeper*, *supervisor*, and *guardian*. A stewardess or steward receives valuable things and protects and nurtures them to make them grow. That is who I am. That is what I do. And that is what I continually attract in my life: valuable things that I can grow. It is vital to learn who you are and become more and more of that each day. Identify your *being*, then look up some synonyms for that identity. Embody those words and you will see them manifest themselves in your life.

The longer we travel through life without identifying who we are, the more opportunities we may squander. Iyanla Vanzant explained how her journey to identify more of her *being* came to the forefront when she began to work with Oprah Winfrey. Think about that: By the time Iyanla met Oprah, she had already written thirteen books and traveled the world as a spiritual teacher. But she had not yet fully connected with the part of her *being* that affirmed her self-worth. Just as she was facing the most abundant opportunity of her life, she had to go through the process of learning to connect better with her *being*. She would later explain that her regrettable decision to sever her business-relationship with Oprah came from failing to identify her self-worth and value.

Most of us would want to have that all figured out by the time we met Oprah Winfrey, but Iyanla's process happened right in the middle of her groundbreaking moment. Even though she wasn't fully prepared for the moment, her extraordinary gifts ushered her into great abundance. If you are an extraordinarily gifted person like Iyanla, your gifts may take you into abundance faster than your internal work has prepared you for. But don't worry. Follow where life is leading you, but do this knowing that connecting with your *being* will eventually become a process you will have to engage in.

The main reason you want to identify your *being* is so you can become more of what you want. Your job is not to search for what you want (abundance), but to become an open door through which abundance can flow. Your ultimate job is to *become* something beautiful, not just to have beautiful things. Being abundance internally will generate abundance externally. Being peaceful internally will generate peace externally. On the other hand, being fearful internally will generate terror externally. But if you become more of who you are, then beauty will have no choice but to make its home with you. The way to become beautiful is to know who you really are and live that out. The beauty is already there. You were born with it.

Doing

Doing is the process of taking actions to express your *being*. As I said, I operate as a stewardess. Therefore, I take certain external actions to express that. A steward masters actions like saving and investing to make money grow. There is internal and external work happening with that: I am acknowledging and developing my inner steward while aligning my external actions to facilitate that. It is the combination of the right internal work with the right external work that will produce the energy of abundance we need.

Essentially, what I do is dictated by who I am—my *doing* comes out of my *being*. Your *doing* must come out of your *being* as well. Identify who you are and take the external actions that align with that. If you are a hunter, be more and more of a hunter every day! Hunters can enjoy the thrill of trying new, more risky financial adventures. It is fun for hunters to "grind" and "hustle"; feeding off the adrenaline of life motivates them. If that is who you are, don't snuff that out! Embrace your inner hunter! There are countless people with that same spirit who are financially successful.

Bill Gates is one of the richest people alive, and he is a hunter. He is most well known for being one of the world's savviest technology geniuses, and for being a generous philanthropist. But in his early days of running Microsoft, his competitors referred to him as "a killer." While developing his iconic company, Gates later recalled, every night before going to bed he was consumed with thinking, "What have I not thought about?" His hunt for success and his astute ability to engage with his competitors led him to where he is today: one of the wealthiest and most influential businessmen of our generation. Gates honed his inner hunter to become an icon in global business.

If you're a hunter, develop your *being* by trusting your instincts more, by managing your money in ways that suit your thrill-seeking temperament. I have a friend who I've identified as a hunter, but he hasn't identified with that yet. He has all the right instincts of a hunter, but he hasn't stopped to connect with that and learn how to flow with it. His instincts are telling him he should be putting his money to greater use, and they are right.

Your money should be moving, working—always doing something productive. Money sitting stagnant is like food left uneaten: it's just going to rot away. Inflation will eat away at it faster than interest will increase it. Hunters know the value of being financially aggressive, but they also know when to be still and quiet at the right times. My advice to all my hunters out there: Add wisdom and knowledge to your instincts. Learn what your investment interests are—what is your tolerance level for risk? Read books that speak to your inner hunter; shadow mentors who have embraced their own hunter spirit. And pray. Get quiet and ask for what you want. Let God help you work out the details. You will have so much fun gaining your abundance while walking in line with your *being. Doing* is done best when it's done from your *being.*

Having

Being + Doing = Having *Abundance*

Having is the tangible result of who you are (*being*) and what actions you take (*doing*). Who you are and what you do will attract results—and this will translate into what you will have. Many people are motivated to have more and more, but we should be primarily motivated by *being* rather than *having*. The people who practice the energy of abundance are rarely motivated by just having more money. They know more money will come, and they are primarily motivated by being abundance-minded. And not just in the area of finances—people who walk in the energy of abundance are enjoying abundance in all areas of their lives. Remember, true abundance is having an ample amount of *all* that we need, not just money.

By tapping into their inner abundance, they can pursue meaningful endeavors without having to worry about whether the money will come. These people pursue and nurture fulfilling relationships; they reject relationships that won't be fulfilling. They pursue meaningful financial opportunities; they reject opportunities that won't feed their souls. They have enjoyed money in such abundance that they don't need to jump at any and every opportunity to get it. *Having* more money is a natural result of just *being* who they are. These people define themselves not by what they have but by who they are—because they know that who they are will produce what they end up having.

On the other hand, we have all known of people who define themselves by what they have, to their detriment. Their *being* is wrapped up in it. I recently saw an advertisement that asked people to describe the most meaningful lessons they'd learned about money. Most of them said that learning to separate their identities from their debt was a milestone for them. Think about that: these precious people began to define their identities by the amount of debt they had. Not by the amount of success they had, or the amount of value or virtue they had—but by the amount of debt they had. They explained that they experienced embarrassment and shame about their debt, some so severely that they even contemplated suicide. This is why we cannot allow our *beings* to become defined by what we have—because wealth can fluctuate unpredictably, and that is too shaky of a foundation to judge ourselves by.

A study published in the August 2013 issue of the *Journal of Personality and Social Psychology* found that wealthier participants were more likely to link their identities with their money. They even believed that wealth was a part of their genetic makeup, and that they were entitled to more wealth because their genes predisposed them to it! The problem with this logic is that it gives money too much power over *being*. What would it mean if those people lost their wealth? It would communicate that something was wrong with them, even down to their genes! It would be understandable, then, for a person with such a money-centered identity to experience suicidal thoughts and feelings in the face of financial difficulties.

Our *being* comes out of our hearts, so when we define ourselves with money, we are wrapping our hearts up in money. That is very dangerous, as we can see. We must learn to have and use money without allowing its presence or absence to become a part of who we are. You will enjoy plenty along your journey toward abundance, so learn to be okay with whatever you have at the moment while you're on your way to more. Whether you have a little or a lot, you must find your power in your *being*. Remember, *having* is just the result of *being* and *doing*. It is not your identity.

Let me make an important point here: even if you have not yet connected with your *being*, your external actions will still produce results. For example, if you haven't yet discovered that you are a steward but you have been saving and investing, you will still produce good results. *Doing* will always produce results, even if you have not yet identified your *being*. But combining your *being* with *doing* will produce *abundant* results, and that's what we're after. When I was in my early twenties, I had no idea who my *being* was. I had been taught to save, so that's what I did—and I still reaped wonderful results from those actions. But once I understood who I was, I could take those actions with more purposeful intention, which produced more abundant results.

The first step on our journey to abundance is to realize how valuable we are, because value will attract value. Once you've accepted that you are worth all of the abundance the world has to offer, then your energy and actions will draw more of that abundance to you. It's not a matter of wishful thinking but of really believing what is true about yourself and taking actions that align with that. The next chapter of the book unveils the blueprint for how to take more meaningful actions with the value you've discovered. This blueprint is the most essential component of your journey to abundance.

True Abundance is having an
ample amount of all that we need.

CHAPTER 3

The Blueprint for Abundance: Triggers

Success at anything meaningful will come with challenges, and many of those challenges are in our own psyches. We hold beliefs that obstruct our paths toward abundance, and it's time to call those obstructions to the surface. Identifying and confronting these obstacles will clear the path for you to walk in abundance more smoothly. I have been practicing the energy of abundance for seventeen years, and my experiences have shown how important it is to rid ourselves of the mental and emotional goop that gets clogged in our systems. A clogged pipe slows down the flow, and if it goes unattended, the flow will eventually stop altogether. We don't want our abundance to slow down or stop, and we can follow this blueprint to clear out our minds:

1) Identify the triggers that present obstacles for you.
2) Saturate yourself in the truths necessary to heal those triggers.
3) Express gratitude for your current and future success.
4) Finally, go and live your life enjoying abundance.

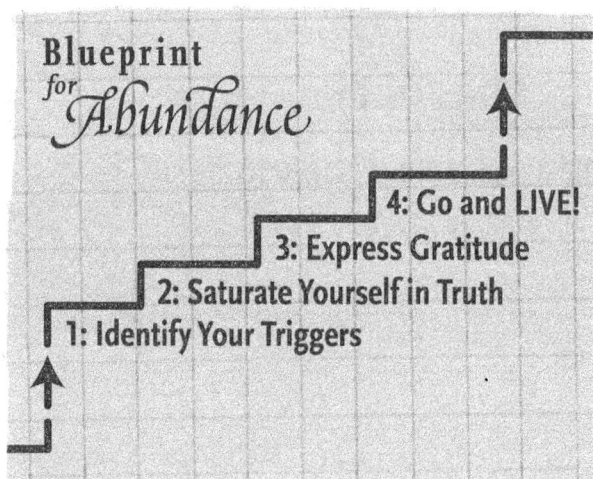

What Is a Trigger?

The most powerful inner work we can do is to heal.
Whatever deficiencies we have are usually due to a wound
that needs healing. We have all had negative experiences
with money that have defined many financial actions
we've taken (or failed to take). I refer to those experiences
as triggers. A trigger can be a specific event, a particular
person—any experience that sparks fear and pain in our
psyches about money. Fear and pain will always create
barriers to success.

I had such an experience as a teenager that became
a trigger for me. When I was in high school, one of my
good friends once gave me five dollars for lunch. A few
days went by and we got into a silly argument about something at school. While we were arguing in the cafeteria,
in front of thirty of our schoolmates, she yelled, "And you
still owe me five dollars I gave you for lunch!"—implying

that I was too poor to afford my own lunch and that if she hadn't helped me, I would've starved or something. At least that's how I interpreted her statement. The embarrassment I felt came out of nowhere. I didn't expect to feel that way about what she said. But it made me so angry that I punched her, something I deeply regret.

I learned something about myself that day: I hate feeling indebted to people. Being in someone's debt makes me feel inferior. I now know that this inferiority complex stems from my ego, not from my *being*. My *being* can relax and be comfortable in any situation. But my ego can get all stirred up about many things, and feelings of indebtedness is one of them. The feelings I felt during that fight are a trigger for me. Over time, they deceptively convinced me that I could not allow myself to have a need that I couldn't fulfill on my own—that I could only rely on myself, because everyone else was waiting to hold their help over my head.

You can probably imagine how much stress a person experiences when she can't rely on anyone but herself. She will live under a lot of pressure to make sure she does not have to reach out to anyone for help. She will create a lonelier experience for herself because of this trigger. The trigger can begin as embarrassment, but it will develop into shame. It can affect how you feel if your savings dwindle. It can affect how optimistic you can be about the future. It can affect your ability to trust in relationships. It will become a monster. Triggers like this are soft spots that spark fear in us, and they block our way to abundance. They need to be identified and then healed.

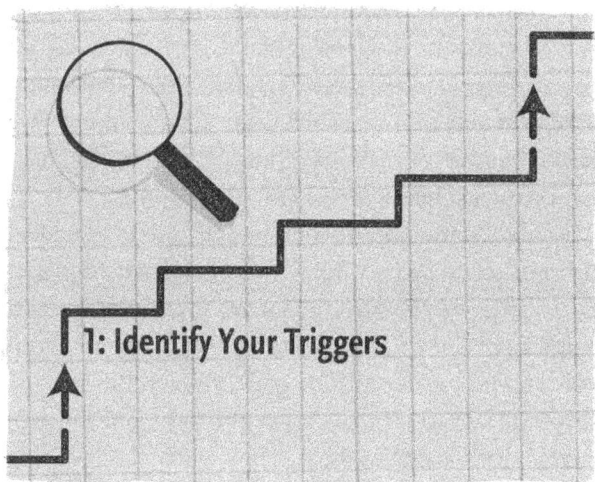

1: Identify Your Triggers

Step 1: Identify Your Triggers
There are all kinds of experiences that can become triggers. Everyone has at least one that plays a major role in how he or she interacts with money. I have a friend who experienced malnutrition as a child while growing up in poverty in a single parent household. That experience has become a trigger for her, because it sparks fear in her about money.

A trigger can begin as embarrassment – it will develop into shame.

That trigger has also led to some very troubled relationship decisions. She has had difficulty connecting in relationships, because she needs her partners to prove their love by providing for her financially. Although it is perfectly healthy to show love using money, it had become an unhealthy need for her, one that defined her relationships. She was always anxious that her partners would leave her holding the bag and she would end up in poverty again. She stayed too long in abusive relationships because she became dependent on her partners' financial provision. Because of her trigger, she didn't feel safe in the world. She placed herself in unhealthy situations to capture the feeling of safety she lost as a child.

In matters of money and matters of love, failing to identify a trigger will lead you far away from the life of abundance you've always desired. So then how do you determine what your triggers are? You can start by taking stock of your emotions and decisions. It will take some practice to become aware of your emotions at a time when you're acting out of fear, but it's work well worth doing.

Part of the process of connecting with your *being* is to take a look at your life and notice where you're experiencing pain. Then you should examine what decisions you've made to actually prolong that experience. To do this, you must get very honest about your feelings. When you notice yourself growing anxious about something, stop and take inventory of why you feel that way. Let's use the example of accepting a loan from a friend. If you find that you feel fear and shame when deciding whether to accept the loan, it might mean that indebtedness is one of your triggers. So, when you notice that you're feeling this kind of pain, you can confront your feelings by talking them out with yourself:

Why am I afraid to accept this loan? I don't think my friend is trying to take advantage of me in any way. She hasn't displayed any untrustworthiness in our friendship to justify my fear. So... what am I afraid of? I have that memory from high school again. Maybe I don't want to lose this friendship over money. More than that, I don't want this person to embarrass me about this loan. This is my trigger, stepping in to protect my ego. But if I allow that, it will hold me back from a good financial opportunity. Thanks, Ego, but I've got this. There is nothing to be afraid of.

A mental process like this involves closely connecting with your *being*. Your feelings are always a good place to start. If you notice yourself feeling a painful emotion, get with yourself and talk it out, or discuss your feelings with a friend who knows you well. If you're being honest, your trigger will reveal itself. One-on-one consultations can be used to coach clients on identifying their triggers. This process will help remove blockages to abundance.

Your Trigger Is Not a Flaw

It is important to avoid viewing your trigger as a flaw. It's better to think of it as a soft spot. Be gentle with yourself. Identifying your triggers is an opportunity for you to heal, not an opportunity to beat yourself up. It's a chance to find out where you've been nicked, cut, and bruised. Show compassion to those areas and pour love on them. A trigger is like a "boo-boo." If a child comes to you and shows you a boo-boo, you wouldn't reprimand the child for having it. You would say "Oh my gosh, are you okay? Let me help you." We even go as far as to kiss boo-boos! In the same way, you should have compassion toward your own triggers. They are the things that have hurt you, and there are no better healing salves than compassion and love. After you've identified a trigger, immediately start the healing process: saturate yourself in truth.

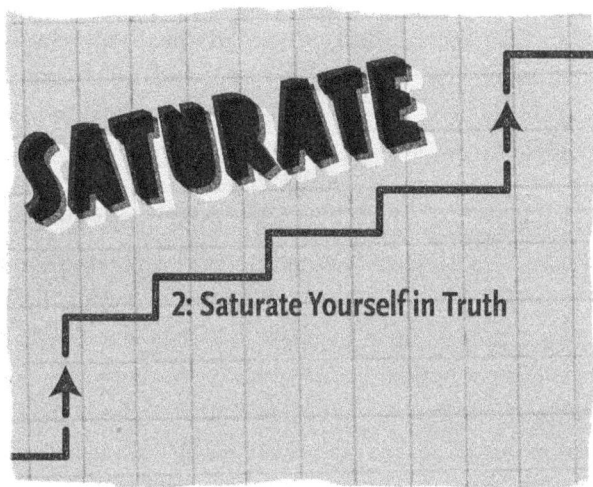

2: Saturate Yourself in Truth

Step 2: Saturate Yourself in Truth

The way to heal a trigger is to *saturate yourself in truth*. The definition of saturate is to *drench, douse,* or *soak*—to *pour it on* in abundance! That is what you need to do with your triggers: saturate them in truth until the fear is drowned out and only healing remains. The truth will hold the compassion and love that you need to heal. With healing comes the clarity and confidence you need to make sound financial decisions.

Many successful people employ the saturation process to heal wounded areas of themselves. I have great admiration for the platform of relationship coach Derrick Jaxn. He uses his internet influence to speak to women about growing in self-love. In one of his Facebook Live videos, he shared that he struggled to develop confidence in his speaking career. He didn't like the way he pronounced certain words, and he wondered if people even cared to hear what he had to say. Because he'd decided he wanted to be a motivational speaker regardless, he adopted a saturation process. He explained how he spent fifteen minutes of each day saying affirmations about his speaking abilities. He would say to himself in the mirror, "I'm a king. What I have to say is valuable. Even if it doesn't come out perfectly, it still matters and it will impact millions of lives." He decided that the area of his speaking abilities needed to be saturated in the truths that would heal him and propel him to success—and that is exactly what I want you to decide.

When you saturate yourself in truth, you are acknowledging that there are realities in your life that contradict what your trigger is trying to communicate to you. If the trigger derives from a uniquely painful experience in the past, saturate yourself in the truth that the experience you had is not likely to ever repeat itself, and is certainly not likely to recur in the intensity with which you previously experienced it. Since my high school experience, I've never had a friend disrespect me over money. In fact, all of my friends have been very generous and wise in their financial dealings with me. They have been blessings to work and serve with. When you saturate yourself in those kinds of truths, then your triggers start to heal. Truthfully, you are now more than capable of handling any pain you may experience with love and grace rather than with feelings of fear or shame.

If we don't heal our triggers, they will block our ability

to experience abundance—not only financially, but in relationships, in health, in business, and so on. When I realized that we could be healed of these fears and move more quickly toward abundance, I became obsessed with identifying and saturating them. I paid closer attention to the triggers of the people in my life and how to help heal them. Here are some triggers I came across and how they can be healed with the truth. Determine if any of them are like your own triggers and think of some truths to speak to heal yourself.

Trigger Types

Childhood Poverty

This is a common trigger. Some people who grew up in impoverished environments have many fears about money. I explained my friend's experience of malnutrition as a child. That experience is unlikely to ever repeat itself. In fact, my friend has enjoyed an abundance of healthy food every day of her life since then. Her ability to eat freely has never since been threatened, so any current fear about that is unnecessary.

Since that's the case, it's important to confront the real monster: that her current fear is not what it once was. Originally, it was a fear of not having enough food. Over time, it has grown into the fear of not having enough of anything! That is what triggers do: they bloom from a tiny seed into a full-grown tree of frightening fruit! Triggers originate from an initial experience, but they feed off lies that have no basis in current reality.

To heal, my friend must saturate herself in the truth
that not only has she never experienced that level of
poverty since, but she has enjoyed an abundance of
life's resources. She can enjoy even more abundance if
she acknowledges that she no longer needs her fear to
protect her from poverty. She is fully capable of gaining
and maintaining wealth. She can let go of fear and walk
in abundance. Once she has saturated in these truths, she
can face her financial situations with more confidence.
She will be more poised to take meaningful financial
actions, which will allow her to enjoy more of the abundance she desires.

She no longer has to subject herself to unhealthy
patterns of behavior in relationships either. She can
envision more of her own value and move away from
dependency on others. She formerly engaged in unconscious patterns of behavior in relationships because of

her fear, and the way to overcome them is to make them conscious by talking them out. When you speak truth to your fears, you convert them from unconscious fears into conscious truths.

> *Triggers originate from an initial experience, but they feed off lies that have no basis in current reality.*

Stinginess

Stinginess is the selfish withholding of resources from others to keep all for yourself. We've already established that being tightfisted with money is not likely to produce more of it, and this is what a stingy person experiences repeatedly, reinforcing his or her stinginess.

I know a man who has worked hard over his lifetime operating businesses and investing wisely. He has amassed a good amount of wealth, but he accomplished this by financially abandoning his children. He barely provided any financial support for them during their lifetimes. As adults, some of his children attempted to renew relationships with him, but he felt they only wanted to reconcile with him so they could gain access to his money. Because of that belief, he not only continued to withhold financial support from them but also repelled any attempts at having relationships with them. The guilt he felt for failing to provide for them tricked him into believing that all they ever really wanted was his money, so he became more and more stingy toward them.

By rejecting these connections, he only reinforced his
fear that people only cared about him for his money. He
pushed the away the people who wanted a genuine relationship and ended up attracting people who did only
have greed in mind. In this way, he created the energy
that communicates to the universe that he values his
money over relationships. As a result, he continues to
have plenty of money and no meaningful relationships.
This is not abundance. Remember, abundance is having
an ample amount of *all* that we need. If we have plenty
of money and not much of anything else, then we are
actually quite poor.

To heal his trigger, the truth this man needs to saturate
himself with is the fact that abundance does not respond
well to stingy energy. Money is a servant that wants to be
used to enrich relationships, not repel them. The truth
is, he needs to forgive himself for not providing for his

children and ask for their forgiveness. The truth is, he places too much value on money. He has allowed money to cost him his children, and that is too high a price to pay for anything. The truth is that he has developed his identity around money, and therefore he believes that if he gives any of it away, he is giving himself away. The truth is that the very people he is withholding his money from are the people who will end up inheriting it anyway. This trigger will be painful to heal, but it's worth it, because this healing can vastly improve this man's overall quality of life.

When he is able to heal, he will start to experience life in ways he never could have imagined. He will learn how beautiful life can be when he opens his heart to his children, and when he realizes how cheap money is compared to love. When he is able to heal, the universe will respond to his healing by manifesting his new desires for love and relationship. Who knows? Perhaps he will gain not only his children but also his grandchildren and great grandchildren—a whole new family.

Overestimating

Overestimating the negative power of money is the exaggerated belief that money can do more harm than good. It usually stems from witnessing someone close to you develop an addiction that relies on money—such as a gambling, shopping, or drug addiction. With this trigger in your psyche, you will respond to money the same way you respond to anything you're afraid of: by avoiding it. If you want more abundance, this trigger must be healed. We've all heard the saying "The *love of money* is the root of all evil." But this saying has been commonly misperceived

to be "*Money* is the root of all evil." The subtle omission of the word "love" completely warps the meaning of
the saying. (The subtle omission of love is probably the
real root of all evil!) If you've believed the misconception
that money is the root of all evil, then you're certainly
going to drive it away. You've bought into the misbelief
that money will cause more harm than good, and that is
simply not true.

I recently read an article in *Borgen Magazine* that said
it would take only five billionaires to end world hunger.
It is fascinating to imagine that it would take only five
people to heal the world in that way! That would certainly
not be an evil way to use money. In fact, that would be
the most wonderful way money had ever been used in
human history! Money can be used for all kinds of good,
so it's not wise to believe that money is evil. Yes, falling in
love with money will cause all sorts of evils: greed, deceit,

abuse, stinginess, etc. Falling in love with money means that you have identified yourself with it, and people will go to great lengths to protect their identities, even to the point of committing evils. Don't fall in love with money—it won't respond well to that energy. But don't avoid money either. Find the balance that can allow you to enjoy it in a healthy manner.

I had a friend whose trigger was overestimation. She would regularly ask to borrow forty dollars at the end of the month because her income was not stretching to her next paycheck. After a few months of giving her the money, I suggested that we develop a budget for her, because it should be easy to find forty extra dollars in her income. We discussed which expenses she should use cash for and which ones she should use a credit card for. She was in her early twenties and needed to establish a credit history anyway, so I suggested she put a small expense on her credit card each month. This would eliminate the need for her to borrow $40 each month, and it would allow her to build her credit history and improve her credit score.

When I suggested she use a credit card, her eyes bulged open and she gasped, "Oh no! I don't want to use a credit card! I don't want to become addicted to using it!" She felt that the temptation to abuse credit cards would be so strong that she couldn't risk using them at all. Although it is a good idea to be cautious when using credit cards, it's not a good idea to avoid them completely. Her fear was an overestimation of money's power. I explained to her that there was no reason to be afraid, that she should trust her ability to be wise and prudent. Isn't it better to practice using them wisely than to miss out on the convenience they can offer?

Her fear of the power of money (or credit cards, in this instance) was holding her back from receiving a measly forty dollars each month! If fear can keep her from receiving forty dollars, it will certainly keep her from receiving real abundance. If it can hold her back from a little, it will find a way to hold her back from a lot. Essentially, her problem was inexperience. She just had not had enough life experience to learn to trust herself with money and credit cards.

Over time, she saturated herself in some truths in order to become less fearful about money's ability to control her. The truth is, money is not evil and it is not the root of all evil. Remember that money is a servant to us, and it can be used for good. It responds well to being used for good. Credit and money are tools the universe uses to meet our needs. The truth is, money is not more powerful than you are. You are fully capable of using money and credit without losing control.

If you've believed the misconception that money is the root of all evil, then you're certainly going to drive it away.

Indebtedness

This is my own trigger. Whenever I feel a sense of indebtedness, fear and shame surface in an attempt to impede my progress toward abundance. I start trying to protect my ego from embarrassment. In the past, I've missed good financial opportunities because of this trigger.

I can easily spot indebtedness taking effect in someone else, and I've noticed it manifest in one of my close relatives. He was in financial need after a crisis with the IRS, and his situation was so urgent that he had no choice but to ask to borrow money. Because I love him, I offered to give him a monetary gift rather than the loan he requested. I didn't want him to have to worry about paying money back to the IRS *and* to me. I made it clear that I did not expect to be paid back. He accepted the gift and that was that—or so I thought.

We had previously enjoyed a very fun relationship, so I fully expected to continue having fun together as usual, but I began to notice that he was becoming distant. He stopped answering or returning my calls, and if I managed to get hold of him, he would immediately say that he was working on paying me the money back and that he needed more time. That was the last thing I was expecting to hear from him, because I thought I had made it clear that I didn't expect repayment. But in his mind, I had given him a loan that he had to *quickly* repay. I was shocked! The sense of indebtedness tricked him out of the enjoyment of a free gift. Sadly, I can understand exactly how he felt. He could no longer enjoy a relationship with me, because all I reminded him of was a debt he owed.

I had an astonishing realization from this experience: there are some people you cannot have *any* type of financial relationship with until they heal their triggers. I attempted to give him a gift in order to spare him the pressures of a loan, but he took on those pressures anyway. From that point forward, I could not offer him loans or gifts because of the way this trigger affected him. If this trigger could prevent him from receiving free gifts, how much more do you think it was preventing him from receiving the abundance that his heart desires?

This is why it is so important to heal your triggers: they will block you from receiving the goodness that is being provided for you. The truth to saturate this trigger with is that you can trust the people who love you to give generously to you without holding debt over your head. Truthfully, it's not shameful to have needs. In fact, having a need is an opportunity for the universe to demonstrate how loved and cared for you are.

This advice may be particularly difficult for men to accept, because of the traditional male dominance in financial matters in our society. Gender roles have discouraged males from being financially dependent, especially on women. The good news is that such roles are changing as women are increasingly earning more than their male partners and men are becoming more comfortable assuming homemaker responsibilities. But studies still show that both men and women have retained the idea that men should be providers. This transition period in gender roles may be sending mixed messages to men, making them feel more comfortable asking for loans but still uncomfortable with accepting financial gifts.

Indifference

Having strong feelings about money is not always healthy, but neither is having no feelings at all about it—not if you're ready for abundance. Indifferent people have no thoughts about how they are managing their money, where it is going, where it is coming from, how to use it, and so on.

Everyone wants abundance, but an indifferent person just doesn't want it badly enough to do the mental and emotional work we've discussed. Or occasionally they'll have ambition toward abundance, but the urge will quickly fall away. Indifference usually stems from always having enough money, so much so that you never had to think about it—usually because your parents were wealthy during your childhood or you had relationship partners who assumed most of the financial responsibilities.

One of the ways indifference can block your abundance is by reinforcing your reliance on someone else. Two of my clients told me that they feel indifferent about building wealth because they know they can depend on inheritances from their parents and grandparents. One client is a young working woman who doesn't budget, save, or invest for her retirement because she is confident that the inheritances will provide adequate financial support for her in the future. The other client is close to retirement age and has not built any equity in her retirement account because she is counting on receiving an inheritance from a parent. Both of those mindsets are certainly hindering their paths toward their own abundance, but even more risky is the possibility that they may not receive as much inheritance money as they expect.

Many studies have confirmed that Americans are enjoying a longer life expectancy. The percentages of people living longer past retirement age has been gradually rising from 8 percent in 1950 to 12 percent now, and it's expected to reach 20 percent by 2050. One out of every ten women and one out of every twenty men will live past one hundred years old! The likelihood is that people will be spending more of their retirement savings to live past their working years, and that means less of an inheritance will be left over after they die.

Now, that is good news for retirees who have abundance—they can expect to live and enjoy their money longer—but it's bad news for the people who are indifferent toward building their own wealth because they are relying on inheritances. Although I think it's a wonderful blessing to have wealth in your family that you can look forward to, I wouldn't recommend ditching your own abundance in reliance on someone else's. Feeling financially secure is an important need everyone should be able to enjoy, but you should use that security to motivate you to pursue your own destiny and abundance, rather than allowing it to stifle that pursuit.

Another way indifference can block your abundance is by causing you to overlook it. Liken this to relationships: if you have valuable people in your life but you're indifferent toward them, you will fail to show appreciation for them. You will overlook their value and fail to nurture them or help them grow. If valuable people are being treated this way, *they will leave*. The universe will move them to a place where they can flourish in the way they were created to flourish. They will not stick around to be ignored, neglected, or abused. Abundance is the same way. It deserves to be noticed and appreciated, but the indifferent person is either unable or unwilling to do so.

All indifference isn't bad or wrong. At times, people have good reasons to be indifferent about money. Maybe they are on a financial level they can easily maintain and are content with that. Or they are at a point in life when doing the internal and external work to pursue abundance is just too much for them right now. Maybe they've recently gone through a major life change like divorce, a new marriage, the birth of a child, or a new job. Their focus needs to be on another area of life, and doing the work I've been describing is just not a priority. That's perfectly okay. But if you are ready for abundance and you're noticing that your drive toward it is a bit on the lazy side, you can heal this trigger with some truth saturation.

Even I have struggled with feelings of indifference on my financial journey. I was once given the opportunity to embark on a real estate venture. I was given almost unlimited access to the mind of a very successful businesswoman who generously taught me what she knew about real estate. She didn't even charge me a fee for her time, which was abundance in itself. A person with her expertise could have easily billed me for her time and information and I would have paid. So I was very fortunate to have access to it without having to pay for it.

After I had all the tools and information I needed, all that was left to do was to get started on the deal—but I found myself putting it off. I wasn't making the calls or setting the appointments required to get the ball rolling. I always found a good reason to do something else besides work on this deal. I felt like I was being lazy or ungrateful for not acting on all that precious information my real estate friend had given me. What was my problem? I'd lost interest in the venture and didn't want to do the work required to succeed in it, but I didn't understand why. I needed to do some connecting with my being and saturate myself in some truth to figure it out.

What I discovered was that although I admire my friend's real estate prowess, it wasn't an area that I had passion for. The hustle and bustle of it, the travel required, and the financial risk didn't really suit my temperament. Although it was a great deal for someone else, it wasn't the right deal for me, and that's why I became indifferent toward it. My indifference wasn't bad or wrong; there was a reasonable explanation for it. But I didn't allow it stop my pursuit of abundance. I sought out other financial ventures that did suit my personality.

My point is that if you notice you're being indifferent about something that is important to you, connect with your *being* and identify the trigger. After that, move on toward your abundance in a way you can enjoy. Perhaps you're indifferent about abundance right now because the work seems too daunting? If so, take a bite-sized approach to it. Instead of focusing on doing all the internal work, just focus on the part you like the most. For example, start by just connecting better with your *being* and don't worry about identifying your triggers yet. Or focus on mastering one of the external actions without worrying about the internal work yet. This is your journey. Take it at whatever pace you want without losing complete interest in having abundance.

Indifference can block your Abundance by causing you to overlook it.

Vampires

Vampires are the people in your life who drain you of your energy and resources. They can be huge obstacles to abundance. These people are the takers in your life: the relatives who ask for exorbitant financial gifts or loans without ever repaying; the friends who never have any money but always ask you to go out, leaving you to pay the tab; the relationship partners who are indifferent, stingy, or have their own triggers they are not actively working to heal. People can be our greatest blessings or our biggest obstacles in life, and it's up to us to identify them properly.

I've had experiences with all sorts of vampires, and frankly, I am glad I did. I'm grateful that the universe presented me with the opportunities to learn the "people lessons" I've learned. I've had relatives who viewed my financial success as their own personal piggy bank. They had a sense of entitlement to my money simply because we are related. It is a huge mistake to allow other people to maintain a sense of entitlement to your success. I made that mistake. I allowed people to make me feel that I owed them something just because the universe was good to me. I felt obligated to give when I didn't want to give. The only thing this did was drain my bank account and my emotional energy.

When you realize you have to break this cycle, it will be difficult. You will have to change people's expectations of you based on the value you place on yourself. Sending the message "You are entitled to my stuff" is not a loving message for you. It obligates you to people without any real substance. You may come to realize that some people are more interested in having access to your stuff than they are in having access to you—your heart and soul. And that is what we really want from our relationships: heart and soul. It will take courage, but you must change the expectation. And yes, the people who are only interested in your stuff may disengage from you. But not everything you lose is a loss—because others who are more interested in loving you will end up engaging with you more deeply.

So how do you spot a vampire? All you have to do is listen. A vampire will expose himself by using manipulation. One of the tactics a vampire will use against you is what I refer to as "survivor's guilt." Survivor's guilt is an actual mental condition that occurs when a person believes he or she has done something wrong by surviving a traumatic event when others did not. A vampire will communicate to you that because you have survived and overcome your triggers while he has not yet overcome, you owe him access to your abundance. You will notice this in comments like "Oh, you think you're better than everyone else" or "You haven't always had so much—remember where you came from." Comments like that are designed to make you feel guilty about being, doing, and having the abundance you enjoy.

Don't take the bait! If you allow yourself to experience guilt for having abundance, you will begin to unconsciously drive it away. If you pay close attention, you will notice that others who walk in abundance will never use this tactic toward you. They are going to be happy with your success, because they are happy with themselves. They have encountered the same types of vampires along their journey, and they would never resort to such maneuvers. The vampires who project negative energy toward you are straightforward to deal with: avoid having any type of financial relationship with them until they heal. This can still be tricky, though, because many vampires are family members or fake friends. It's fine to help these people in true emergencies if you want, but outside of that, I would avoid having a financial relationship with a vampire at all costs, regardless of whether it's a relative.

Some vampires are just no good to have around, but others don't intend to be a drain on you. If you have a partner who is draining your financial energy and resources, it is not likely he or she is doing it intentionally. It is more probable that this person has his or her own triggers to heal or financial literacies to learn. It's important that you and your partner share the same values about money, because many studies have consistently confirmed that financial discord is among the top reasons couples break up.

A 2010 article in *Psychology Today*, "Don't Let Money Ruin Your Relationship," suggests that the reason couples experience increasing pressures about financial matters is because they avoid talking about money to avoid the tension. Having a partner who is neither interested in nor willing to communicate with you about money will be a major obstacle to abundance. If you're ready for abundance and your partner seems to have no interest in this, ask him or her to have an open conversation with you about it. Discussing your triggers together can present an opportunity to strengthen your relationship as you learn of each other's past experiences more deeply. Saturating yourselves in truth together will only expand the loving and healing bond that you share. Sometimes, all it takes to get on the same page is a conversation about what's important to you and asking for support. Most times, your partner will be eager to support you, but be prepared to reevaluate any partnership that doesn't line up with your financial goals and dreams.

If you begin to experience guilt for having Abundance, you will unconsciously drive it away.

When it comes to vampires, I've learned that their presence is more about us than it is about them. Sometimes, it's our own pre-existing triggers that attract vampires, and one way to prevent that is to get clearer with the universe. If you notice that you're attracting vampires into your life, it may be because you aren't clear on who your *being* is. When I was attracting vampires, I knew I enjoyed meeting needs, but I didn't get much more specific with the universe than that. I hadn't specifically defined how I wanted to be of service in the world, so I was attracting a lot of random neediness.

If you're a person who enjoys helping people and you're also attracting abundance, then the random neediness will find you. As a result of drawing those vampires into my life, I began to feel used—and this was diminishing the joy I usually experienced from being generous. I had to redefine what I wanted and who I wanted to be. I didn't want to be the person everyone called to help pay their rent or to borrow money for a night at the club. I wanted to meet more meaningful and urgent needs that made a difference in people's lives. I wanted to help people pay their way through college, buy a home, pay an unexpected medical debt, etc. I had to get clear with myself, and so do you.

You are a limited resource, and your resources are valuable. Your time is indispensable, because you can never reproduce time. Your energy and your money are reproducible, but it takes time to reproduce them. They deserve and desire to be planted in good soil, not weak or shallow soil. Once you redefine your value you will attract fewer vampires. Remember, this is your journey, and the people you choose to walk with must add value to it. As an expression of love for yourself, start to notice and heal the vampire relationships you have in your life.

Futurism

If you're a futuristic thinker, you have the gift of fore-sight. You can visualize and strategize about the future. Your keen farsightedness helps you accomplish goals to create the destiny you've already seen in your mind. But if you're not careful, this gift can become a trigger—because a futuristic thinker can also foresee problems, which can cause fear about the future. A futuristic thinker can be in a current state of abundance and still be disturbed by the possibility of less abundance in the future. The irony is that he or she can fail to enjoy current abundance for fear about future abundance!

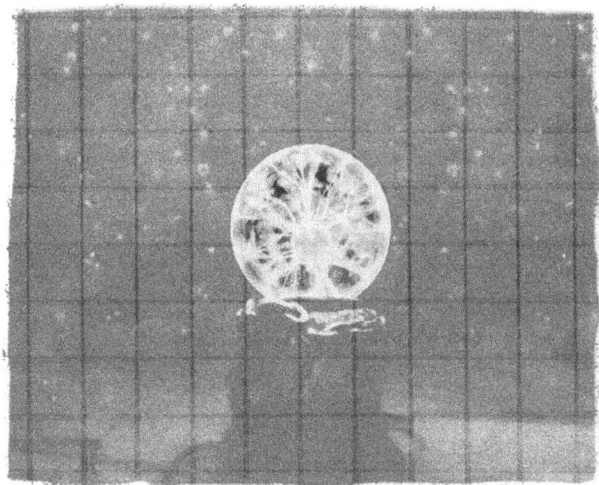

If this is a trigger for you, I want you to realize that you are unnecessarily reaching into the future and bring-ing back pain into the present. This trigger is stealing the joy of your current state of abundance, and it is also stealing from your future, because you are projecting

fearful energy onto your future abundance. It's amazing how the psyche is always preaching that we need to
reach for things to enjoy in life, but as soon as we receive
them the psyche starts preaching that we can't fully enjoy
them because we must worry about the future. Take the
opportunity to connect more deeply with your *being*. Be
determined to heal your psyche by saturating yourself
in the truth that by the time you get to the future, your
abundance will be there. In fact, it is already there waiting for you. The truth is that abundance is attached to
the future—it is one with it. Let's put it this way: if you
have a future, you will have abundance.

Our problem is that we want to have tomorrow today—
but life doesn't work that way. All we can do is what I refer
to as *do the day*—three little words I tell myself when
futurism starts to become a trigger for me. In the present moment, we cannot return to the past to do anything
about previous experiences. In the present moment, we
cannot advance to the future to experience anything there.
We must do the day we have right now. Do this day and
release yourself from the pains of the past and from the
pressures of the future.

Abundance begins as a cosmic thing that you aren't
supposed to be able to calculate. It's something you are
meant to experience with a sense of awe and wonder. The
things we end up being most grateful for are the things
we didn't see coming. Life feels enchanted when you don't
see abundance coming, and it comes at the right place, the
right time, and in just the right amount. It's the timing
of the provision that makes it so beautiful.

I experienced such a provision during the US economic

crisis that began in 2008. The job market at that time was abysmally weak. Jobs were very difficult to find, and the unemployment rate was rising at a historical pace. I had just completed my undergraduate studies at the time and was looking to start my career, but I felt like there couldn't have been a worse time to be a new graduate. I tried to ignore the media when it projected how hopeless it would be to find a good job. I just conducted my job search hoping for the best.

After five months of job hunting, I finally had my prospects narrowed down to three very attractive opportunities. During the interview process, I labeled these jobs as "dream jobs." Although the job market produced greater competition than usual, I was offered two out of the three positions I interviewed for! Think about that: I was offered *two* dream jobs during a job market crisis! I actually had to turn down one dream job to accept the other! What made the situation even more amazing was that my partner was having the same experience at the same time. We both ended up being offered our dream jobs at a time when it was least reasonable to expect that. It was the timing of that abundance that made it such a beautiful experience.

As futuristic thinkers, we must take these kinds of breathtaking memories into account when we start making projections about the future. We can't allow our psyches to convince us that we need to be afraid of anything that's to come. We should allow our memories to convince us that we will have an ample amount of all that we need in the future. It seems ironic, but the best way a futuristic thinker can heal this trigger is to recall truths from the past.

I've named only a few, but there are many more triggers people experience that can hinder their abundance. Once you've taken a mental and emotional inventory of yourself and identified what your triggers are, saturate each one of them in the truth. Remind yourself that your triggers are not flaws, just bruises that need healing. By pouring truth on them, you will show compassion and love to yourself that will heal any triggers you have. Once you begin to practice this part of the blueprint, you'll see all the right doors open for you. In fact, you will *become* the open door to your abundance. When you start to heal, you will feel so grateful that you've discovered how to maneuver your success, your heart will inevitably express gratitude—and that is the next fundamental step in attracting abundance.

CHAPTER 4

Express Gratitude and
GO LIVE LIFE

"Be thankful for what you have; you'll end up having more. If you concentrate on what you don't have, you will never, ever have enough." – Oprah Winfrey

Step 3: Express Gratitude

One of the most successful people of our time, Oprah Winfrey, understands the creative power of expressing gratitude. Gratitude communicates to everything and everyone that you are a safe soul to anchor to. It communicates that you are ready for more. Gratitude comes with a mix of all sorts of delicious ingredients: joy, peace, contentment, relief. With all that yummy energy wrapped up in the expression of gratitude, you become like a sweet-smelling rose when you have a grateful attitude. Who or what would not be instantly attracted to that?

Compare an attitude of gratitude with an ungrateful attitude. Imagine being in a room with someone who has just received a special gift, but she either doesn't notice the gift, doesn't perceive the gift to be special, or has a stinky sense of entitlement toward the gift. Your face would instinctively curl up at the thought of such a bad attitude. Mine too. As a giver, I am always on the lookout for someone to be generous to, but an immediate disqualifier is someone who has an ungrateful attitude. The universe is an even more aggressive giver than we tend to be—actively seeking who to give its abundance to—but of everything we've discussed so far, being ungrateful is the biggest barrier to abundance.

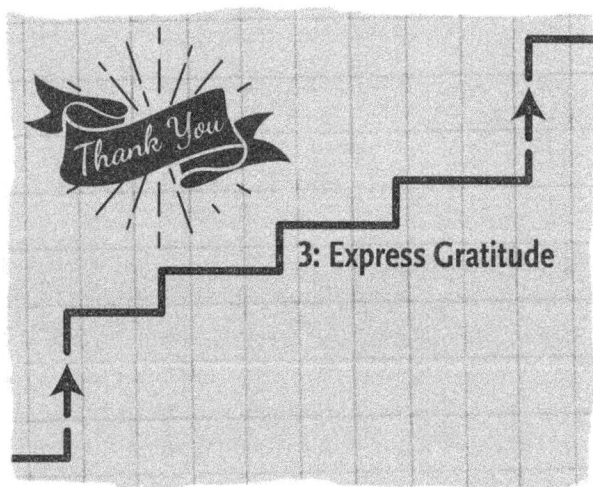

The Gratitude Challenge

If you don't already practice gratitude, I want to challenge you to try being intensely grateful for one week and note how much lighter your energy feels. Letting yourself fall into an attitude of gratitude will give you a new vibe, a new air, a new flair. It will add a coolness and a freshness to who you already are. Moreover, it's likely that the people in your life will benefit from your appreciativeness too. I've learned that anything valuable needs to be recognized and treated as such or you will lose it. It is important to be appreciative of the good things and good people in your life, so I want you to become an expert at noticing, appreciating, and rewarding value. Too often, we only recognize value after we lose it, but we can be wiser than that in our relationships with money and people. We don't have to lose something good before we learn to appreciate it.

Challenge yourself to go to a new level in showing appreciation for your loved ones. Learn their love languages and communicate your appreciation to them in their language. *The Five Love Languages: How to Express Heartfelt Commitment to Your Mate* is a book written by Gary Chapman that describes "five ways to express and experience love." I recommend reading it if you really want to thrive at the gratitude challenge.

A friend of mine regularly uses her wife's love language to nurture their relationship. Her wife's love language is Words of Affirmation, which is the expression of affection through praise, unsolicited compliments, and appreciation through either spoken or written words. Whenever my friend has an opportunity to express gratitude to her wife, she writes her a letter, or leaves her a sweet voice message, or sends her a long, sincere email. Or even better, she takes her out for an intimate dinner and expresses her gratitude face to face. Sure, she could send her gifts or give her big hugs to express her gratitude.

Those types of affection would also be well received. But communicating to her in her particular love language is a more excellent way to the heart—and after all, it's the heart we want. Get creative and take the gratitude challenge! There is a good chance it will enhance all of your relationships.

When you express gratitude, you are communicating to the universe that you want more of what you have. The blueprint for abundance is like the "ask, believe, receive" concept—with gratitude as the "believe" part. *Asking* for your abundance is the step you take when you identify and heal your triggers. *Believing* in your abundance is the step you take when you express gratitude for it before you see it. And then? The only thing left is to enjoy *receiving* your abundance.

Imagine the blueprint another way: there is a garden you want to grow. The first step is to find and plant seeds (identify your triggers). Then, you water them (saturate yourself in truth). Next, expressing gratitude causes the root to take hold in the soil, and this root work is the hidden part of the process that the universe takes care of for you. You've never known a farmer who could attach a root to the soil! That part is when the farmer gets a lot of help from the earth. What's left? The only thing left is to enjoy watching your garden produce a harvest. Gratitude is the glue that connects your work to the work of the universe. Any way you choose to look at it, the process for growth and abundance is working that way. It is built into the fabric of life. The birds show it to us. The garden shows it to us. We see it in ourselves. We see it in others.

This model is a lifelong process, a living model. As we

mature, life will reveal parts of ourselves that need healing. Your soul wants to heal. If you didn't know you had
an illness, your body would want you to know. *Hey, something's wrong here. We're sick. We need healing.* Your body
will start to manifest symptoms to communicate this to
you. It's the same way with any barrier to abundance you
may have. If your soul is so fragmented in this area that
you can't grow and be prosperous, then life will expose
that to you by manifesting symptoms—failed relationships, missed financial opportunities, discontentment,
etc. Life does this so you can see the illness, diagnose
it, treat it, and be healed. Healing is always at the end of
every valuable process.

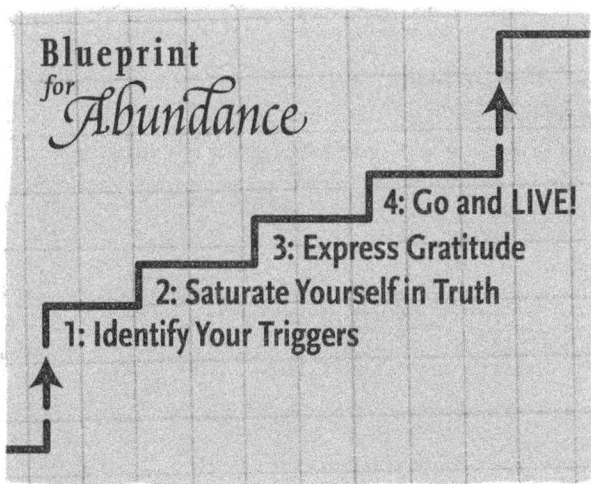

Blueprint
for **Abundance**

4: Go and LIVE!
3: Express Gratitude
2: Saturate Yourself in Truth
1: Identify Your Triggers

Completing one cycle of the process will lead you into
another, and the cycle will begin again in new and more
stunning ways. As you grow, you will learn new truths to
saturate yourself in. You will have new reasons to express

gratitude. You'll flow through the process more quickly and with more peace. Perhaps when starting out, it takes you a week to settle your energy down about a financial situation. But as you practice this, soon it will only take you a day, or just hours or even minutes! Eventually, you'll get to the point at which you don't worry at all. In fact, you'll be excited for new chances to watch the universe work for you!

When you experience this feeling, speak it out! Say, "Thank you!" for something right now. This is the easiest step in the blueprint. Feeling the gratitude is the internal work, but saying "thank you" is the external work. Start expressing gratitude now, not only for the healing of your triggers but also to set the stage for your future abundance.

Quotes of Gratitude

Don't just take it from me. Listen to how important gratitude is to some of the most successful people in the world:

"When you are grateful, fear disappears and Abundance appears."
– Tony Robbins

"Social scientists have found that the fastest way to feel happiness is to practice gratitude." – Chip Conley

"Feeling gratitude and not expressing it is like wrapping a present and not giving it." – William Arthur Ward

"Gratitude is the healthiest of all human emotions. The more you recognize and express gratitude for the things you have, the more likely you will have even more to express gratitude for." – Zig Ziglar

"Acknowledging the good that you already have in your life is the foundation for all Abundance." – Eckhart Tolle

"Opportunities, relationships, even money flowed my way when I learned to be grateful no matter what happened in my life." – Oprah Winfrey

"I don't have to chase extraordinary moments to find happiness—it's right in front of me if I'm paying attention and practicing gratitude." – Brené Brown

Step 4: Go and LIVE!

At this point, you've done your internal work. You've made the challenging effort to connect with yourself and identify the triggers that set up barriers to abundance. You've decided you are no longer going to allow fear to block you. You've saturated yourself in the truths that provide healing and confidence along your journey. You've experienced the liberation to move higher in your financial life. And now, you're grateful. You've learned to express gratitude about the past, the present, and the future. The only thing left to do now is LIVE.

Go and LIVE your life! Go relax. Spend time with the people you love. Do the activities you love to do. Heck, go make some love! Go and live your life surrendered to the process you've undertaken. You've done all your internal work, now go and be the person you were born to be. In this step, we can let our hair down and let the universe handle the details. You've earned it, you deserve it, and it's only a matter of time before you and others will begin to witness the abundance you've created.

As you're living and enjoying your abundance, let each step of the process become a part of your second nature. Take a daily inventory of your *being* to see if there are any triggers operating in your life. Always be mindful of the truths taking shape in your situation and apply them. Let gratitude become a part of your personality. Even having the ability to read the words on this page is reason enough to be grateful.

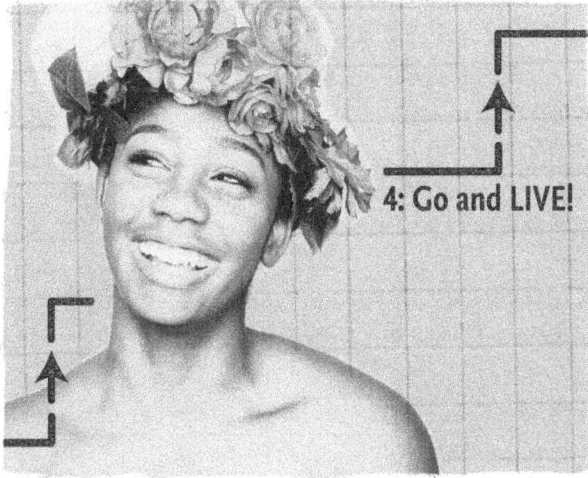

Go and live your life, but be prepared to take some tests. In life, tests always come before progress, so recognize the tests quickly and don't panic. At the very time I am writing this book I am being tested in all of the areas that I am writing about. That's just the nature of life. Challenges are always present to test the quality of the pursuit. While I'm writing this book on abundance, my stocks have taken a very hard hit. While I'm writing about staying in peace, there is a nuisance in my neighborhood frustrating me and my neighbors. While I'm writing this book on self-love, the mistakes I make in relationships, at work, in parenting, etc. seem to be magnified, challenging my confidence. The fact that these things are happening at the very time that I am releasing their counter-energies confirms that they are tests. They are signs that what we're doing is making an impact in the universe.

This encourages me to endure even more vigorously—to hold on even tighter to my self-love, my peace, and my energy of abundance, because I know that by the time you hear from me again, I will have passed all the tests. The outcomes will have settled themselves. These challenges will have shown themselves to be setups for promotion. By the time you hear from me again, my stocks will have rebounded. By the time you hear from me again, the nuisance in my neighborhood will be a distant memory. By the time you hear from me again my self-love will have manifested into more loving relationships with myself and others. Go and live your life with the same confidence that your new internal energy will improve the state of all your affairs.

The final step in the blueprint is to combine all of the internal work we've discussed with the financial basics. It's time to put the heart *and* the hand to work. Walking in abundance is a master course, and practice makes perfect. The external actions you already practice will benefit from the internal work you do—and the internal work is enhanced by learning or reviewing the best external practices. If you haven't been practicing the financial basics, or just need a refresher, then the next chapter will bring you up to speed.

Go and live your life surrendered to the process you've undertaken.

CHAPTER 5

The Externals

In the previous chapters, we discussed the internal actions you need to practice to draw abundance. In this chapter we will discuss the *external* actions that are crucial to financial success. These are the basics of how to handle your money—how to save, budget, invest, etc. Mastering the fundamentals is the best first step toward abundance. If you're already a pro at the externals, then this chapter will contain information you already know, but it may also include useful tips that will take your financial mastery to the next level. If you haven't been practicing the fundamentals, then this chapter will give you some valuable tools to get started.

In the following pages, I will offer you some of the basic tools and practices that have helped me reach financial abundance. I'll also share my experiences so you can avoid some of the pitfalls I encountered along the way. I want to show you how I've combined internal work with my external financial actions, and how abundant the results can be.

Saving: Save and Say

You should view saving as one of the very first bills you should pay—to yourself. Pay yourself first because you've earned it. When I say "pay yourself first" I mean pay your savings account first. On my budget, I list saving as a top expense, and I pay it straight from my paycheck into my savings account. Cultivating the mindset that it is important to pay yourself first reaffirms your value to yourself and to the universe. Sometimes I even say out loud, "I am paying myself first because I am important. I am valuable. I deserve it!" In this way, you align your mind and your hand to practice valuing yourself. I call this the "save and say" method. While you're saving, say something that affirms your value. Speak lovely about your future. Speak kindly about yourself. Create the energy that beckons the servant.

Initially, putting yourself first may feel uncomfortable. Society has done a great job of teaching us that we should build personal equity in misery by placing ourselves last. But if you're anything like me, you've learned that placing yourself last can lead to traumatic results. In the past, I've put myself last in relationships, last at work, last in friendships, last in line—last in almost every area I can think of. And most of those experiences resulted in regrets, wasted time, wasted energy, and wasted resources. I decided to stop building equity in misery by placing myself last and start building equity in abundance by placing myself first. When you place yourself first, you will be able to remain full enough to give to others without becoming depleted. You will find that it is much more satisfying to give from a place of abundance than to give from an empty bucket— and you can use your saving practice to help solidify that.

Don't be afraid to start small. That's what I did in the early days. I decided that 10 percent of my income was a good amount to save. At the time, that meant I saved $60 each paycheck, because my paycheck was $600. I saved that money with pride. I reminded myself that I was doing so because I am important to myself, because my future needs and desires are important too. That internal work of affirming myself combined with that external action worked wonders! Let's just say that shortly after starting this practice, I was able to save a lot more than $60. By the end of that year, I had $10,000 in the bank—more cash than I had ever had at one time! Money just started to flow toward me in unexpected ways. Again, the universe was rewarding me for following the path that was in my soul. It was giving me a nod and a wink for living from my *being*, for speaking goodness out of my mouth, and for using my hand to take prudent action.

Saving Quick-Tip: When you start saving, start with 10 percent of your income each month. If 10 percent is too much, then start with 5 percent. The point is to start the process and build momentum. Practice "save and say" while you're doing the external work. If you can, separate your savings into two accounts—what I call a "touchable" and an "untouchable" savings account. Use money from the touchable account if a minor unexpected expense arises. But never withdraw from the untouchable account unless an extreme emergency arises—which hopefully you will be able to avoid. The untouchable account is the one you'll be most proud of at the end of a year. You'll enjoy the process of adding zero after zero to that account. Try it!

Saving is the first bill you should pay.
Pay yourself first.

Budgeting: The Free Check

Another basic external everyone should practice is budgeting. Budgeting is how you keep track of how much money is flowing in and out. Whether I've had a little or a lot over the years, I've always maintained a budget. Since I'm a steward, budgeting is especially critical for me. I must be able to determine how I've made money increase. If it's not increasing, I need to know why and how to change that.

But regardless of your *being*, budgeting can help you develop strategies to increase your prosperity. It's the only way to calculate whether you're flowing in abundance. If you have a lot coming in and it's all going out, that's not abundance. If you have a lot coming in and only a little going out, that *is* abundance. Keeping a budget can help you track that.

Budgets are simple to set up: you can use a basic Microsoft Excel spreadsheet to catalog your income and expenses. But budgets can be difficult to stick with, because there is an element of discipline required. The best way to develop discipline is to give yourself incentives. Everything is easier with incentive, and I've found a way to incentivize budgeting. I'm going to show you how to get paid big bucks to keep a budget. Things are about to get a bit technical, but if you can stick with me you might be amazed.

Many people are paid biweekly (every two weeks) through their employers. If that is you, then you're in luck, because this system will work easily for you. Let's assume each paycheck is $1,000, and you get two of those each month. When you set up your budget, you should be paying your monthly expenses from the two paychecks you receive each month. So at the end of a normal month, all of your bills will be paid and your paychecks will be spent. You're on to the next month doing the same cycle.

But after about five months, something magical happens: you'll come to a month that has three paydays in it instead of two. I call this month the "magic month," and it happens twice a year. If you've been sticking to your budget, by the time you get to a magic month all of your bills are paid out of your first two paychecks, and you have a whole paycheck left over! I call this extra paycheck the "free check," because you don't have to pay any of your expenses out of it. It's free money! All yours to do whatever you want with! If your paycheck is $1,000, that's $2,000 a year of free money! The universe pays you $2,000 just for sticking to a budget.

The 2019 calendar on the next page shows an example of each payday. The normal paydays are highlighted in blue, while the two free checks are highlighted in stars. Because you can depend on these free checks, you can decide what you want to do with your free money at the beginning of each year: plan a vacation, start a home renovation project, pay off a credit card, save it, or just spend it on shoes! You can start your year off abundance-minded because of this principle!

What is even more amazing is that this principle can be shared with a partner to increase your abundance. If you have a partner who is also paid biweekly and uses this budgeting strategy, you can add his or her free money to your own! If your partner also makes $1,000 per paycheck, that's $4,000 of free money for your household each year!

2019

JAN

S	M	T	W	T	F	S
30	31	1	2	3	4	5
6	7	8	9	10	11	12
13	14	15	16	17	18	19
20	21	22	23	24	25	26
27	28	29	30	31	1	2

FEB

S	M	T	W	T	F	S
27	28	29	30	31	1	2
3	4	5	6	7	8	9
10	11	12	13	14	15	16
17	18	19	20	21	22	23
24	25	26	27	28	1	2

MAR

S	M	T	W	T	F	S
24	25	26	27	28	1	2
3	4	5	6	7	8	9
10	11	12	13	14	15	16
17	18	19	20	21	22	23
24	25	26	27	28	29	30
31	1	2	3	4	5	6

APR

S	M	T	W	T	F	S
31	1	2	3	4	5	6
7	8	9	10	11	12	13
14	15	16	17	18	19	20
21	22	23	24	25	26	27
28	29	30	1	2	3	4

MAY

S	M	T	W	T	F	S
28	29	30	1	2	3	4
5	6	7	8	9	10	11
12	13	14	15	16	17	18
19	20	21	22	23	24	25
26	27	28	29	30	31	1

JUNE

S	M	T	W	T	F	S
26	27	28	29	30	31	1
2	3	4	5	6	7	8
9	10	11	12	13	14	15
16	17	18	19	20	21	22
23	24	25	26	27	28	29
30	1	2	3	4	5	6

JULY

S	M	T	W	T	F	S
30	1	2	3	4	5	6
7	8	9	10	11	12	13
14	15	16	17	18	19	20
21	22	23	24	25	26	27
28	29	30	31	1	2	3

AUG

S	M	T	W	T	F	S
28	29	30	31	1	2	3
4	5	6	7	8	9	10
11	12	13	14	15	16	17
18	19	20	21	22	23	24
25	26	27	28	29	30	31

SEPT

S	M	T	W	T	F	S
1	2	3	4	5	6	7
8	9	10	11	12	13	14
15	16	17	18	19	20	21
22	23	24	25	26	27	28
29	30	1	2	3	4	5

OCT

S	M	T	W	T	F	S
29	30	1	2	3	4	5
6	7	8	9	10	11	12
13	14	15	16	17	18	19
20	21	22	23	24	25	26
27	28	29	30	31	1	2

NOV

S	M	T	W	T	F	S
27	28	29	30	31	1	2
3	4	5	6	7	8	9
10	11	12	13	14	15	16
17	18	19	20	21	22	23
24	25	26	27	28	29	30

DEC

S	M	T	W	T	F	S
1	2	3	4	5	6	7
8	9	10	11	12	13	14
15	16	17	18	19	20	21
22	23	24	25	26	27	28
29	30	31	1	2	3	4

What would you do with $4,000 a year that you didn't have to spend on bills? I hope you're able to find out this year after keeping a budget. Many beginning budgeters need coaching to help them at first. Sometimes the process is too technical to learn solely from a book, so financial coaching services can be a big help.

If you don't get paid biweekly, there is still a tip you can use to help you stick to your budget with incentive: reward yourself every month. When my payment arrangements change, I build an incentive into my budget to keep me motivated. By building a reward system into your budget you will be more motivated to stick to it. As you're listing your expenses into your budget for the month, add an additional expense called "Reward," or whatever cool name you like. See the example of a personal budget on page 78.

Offer yourself a reward for sticking to your budget based on your income. For example, you could list your "Reward" expense at $300. This means that if you stick to your budget and don't overspend for that month, you will give yourself $300 to spend on whatever you want. Seriously, spend it on whatever you want. That massage you've been needing for the past six months? Get it! That really expensive brandy you've been wanting to taste? Drink it! This bonus is a good way to enjoy the rewards of your hard work. Throughout the month, when you're tempted to dig into some of the money you need for your expenses, you'll see your reward there, which should encourage you to stick to the budget. If you don't have $300 for the reward, make it $200 or $100. Find the number that's right for you and use it to motivate yourself. After a while,

MONTHLY BUDGET

EXPENSE NAME	$ COST
Tithe/Giving	200.00
Savings	200.00
Spending Cash	200.00
Groceries	200.00
Gas Utility	50.00
Electric	50.00
Cable/Internet	75.00
Car Insurance	75.00
Cell Phone	50.00
Rent	600.00
Credit Card	50.00
Gym	10.00
Reward	100.00
TOTAL INCOME	2000.00
TOTAL EXPENSES	1860.00
REMAINING CASH	140.00

you will have developed more discipline to budget, and you'll have a few pairs of new shoes to show for it.

The primary purpose of keeping a budget is to help you live within your means and build your abundance. If your expenses are exceeding your income each month, consider reducing the expenses you can reduce or live without altogether. For example, if you find yourself over budget by $100 each month, you should try finding a less expensive cell phone service or cable package. You might even consider canceling cable altogether. You should rarely ever consider reducing your savings or your reward, because those are the expenses that will give you the most incentive to stick with the budget. Don't eliminate your sources of motivation during this process—you'll need those to develop discipline.

Budgeting Quick-Tip: One of the strategies I use each year is to look for ways to increase my income and/or lower my expenses. Every six months, I will review my budget and look for ways to do that. I normally just go line by line on my budget and start doing research and making phone calls asking for lower costs. Once during this process, I was looking for less expensive cell phone service. I happened upon my service provider's website and noticed they were offering the same plan I was currently using for half the price! All I had to do was sign up and my cell phone service cost was cut in half without me losing any benefits. If you can do that with your expenses, you will have more money left over to save, invest, and reward yourself. The key is to develop a mentality that your finances will need a periodic checkup.

Simply keep track of your expenses compared with your

income. The simpler you can keep your budget, the better. The point is to have a solid picture of what you're spending compared with what you're bringing in. Remember, if you get paid biweekly there will be one paycheck during each magic month that you won't need to use for expenses. So if this sample budget reflected a magic month, the total income would be $3,000 instead of $2000. Minus the same $1,860 in expenses, which leaves $1,140 in remaining cash instead of $140!

Tithing/Giving

Tithing is the religious practice of dedicating a tenth (10 percent) of your income to your religious organization. It was designed to ensure that the urgent needs of communities were met and to provide opportunities to demonstrate reverence for God. I can't think of a better combination of internal work and external actions than tithing. It's an external action combined with faith—and faith is an internal work. I've witnessed some of the most beautiful magic in my life surrounding this principle.

   A roommate once noticed that whenever I checked the mailbox, I would gasp out loud because there would be a check for me almost every time. This unexpected income might come in the form of overlooked interest the bank owed me, or a sudden, sharp increase in my equity or my stocks and bonds. It was money that hadn't even been on my radar, and it was just flowing my way. This was happening so often that my roommate asked me what was going on. She didn't tithe, nor was she very interested in religion, so I wondered how I could explain to her that I believed faith combined with tithing was driving this sudden surplus. Since I couldn't think of a round-about way, I just explained it to her as I understood it. I expected her to roll her eyes and dismiss it as religious nonsense, but she didn't. Her eyes opened wide and she said, "That stuff really works, huh?!" She believed me, not only because of what I said, but because of the abundance she was witnessing with her own eyes.

Perhaps you don't tithe, but maybe you're a giver. You lend freely, you give gifts, or you're the person people can call when they have an urgent need. The same energy is at work with that style of giving too. No matter how you choose to share your money, life will find ways to return it to you abundantly.

The universe can't resist giving back to a giver! When you're helping to meet needs, the universe will always repay you in full with interest! If you train your internal energy to enjoy giving, you will be swallowed up in abundance. If you've already been a generous giver, then you can attest this is true. Givers are magnets for abundance, because giving is one of the best ways to practice detachment from money. When money knows it can organically flow to and then through you, it knows you're a safe place to be. It will keep coming back for more of that cool, sweet energy you have.

If you haven't been practicing sharing, giving, tithing, or any form of generosity, I recommend doing so. You can tithe to a religious organization, or find someone every month to give a monetary gift to. Sometimes, instead of tithing, I would ask my friends if they knew anyone who needed anything. I was always able to find someone who was having car trouble, who had just lost a job, or had another urgent need just waiting to be met. I would jump at the chance to help that person, because I knew I would get a double whammy of abundance in return: I would get the personal satisfaction that all humans get from helping each other, and I would also get that gift repaid to me by the universe in some magical way. I couldn't wait to see how it would happen. Giving had become a game that I could enjoy, all the while meeting meaningful needs. I was actually having fun being a giver!

Tithing is an external action combined with faith—and faith is an internal work.

For all my happy tithers out there: Beware! The joy police are out there ready to steal your thunder. We know that negative energy is always waiting to counter positive energy. Even when all you're trying to do is share, there will be forces opposing that. I loved using my tithe to meet urgent needs, but when you're enjoying something good, there is always going to be some rule, some opinion, some technicality that tries to block that.

When I first started tithing, I didn't regularly attend a specific church, because I moved around often due to my service in the US Navy. But I still wanted to practice tithing, both to help other people and to build some financial discipline. So instead of giving to a church, this is one of the times when I would use my tithe to meet someone's urgent need. I would ask people if they needed anything, and I would be amazed when people commented that my asking was the perfect timing for an important need they had. This made me feel special—like God was using me to look out for others. I really enjoyed that feeling, but it wasn't long before negative energy started to creep in to crush that enjoyment.

I started to come across people who would interject and take the fun out of what I was doing. They would say things like "You need to be tithing off the gross and not the net of your income, otherwise it isn't acceptable." Or "You need to tithe off of every financial gift you receive too." Or "You have to give it to a church, not to individuals". These "rules" and "regulations" were just sucking the joy out of me. I didn't even want to give anymore, because I wasn't sure if I was doing it "right" or if it was even meaningful.

This was a good life lesson for me: If your soul is vibing with something good and moving you in the direction of your destiny, there are going to be forces that want to get you off course. You have to learn how to flow in your *being* and enjoy your experience in spite of what naysayers believe. We don't have to stay in between someone else's lines in order to flow with our own *beings*. Let your flow create the lines and boundaries that you follow—not the critics.

Your Credit Score

Your credit score matters—significantly. A master of abundance is always thinking about this three-digit number. Your credit score can cost or save you tens of thousands of dollars—maybe even hundreds of thousands—over your lifetime. I can't stress enough how important it is to diligently work to keep at least a 700-level credit score. This is going to take consistent effort on your part, but it will be worth it when you need to use credit to finance something. I learned this lesson the hard way, and I don't want you to suffer the way I did in order to learn this lesson.

When I was a young adult and had just joined the US Navy, I needed to buy a car. Every nineteen-year-old either needs or wants a car, and I was at that point. Of course, I would need to finance this purchase, since I was just a kid with no cash at all. It was my first time buying a car and I didn't want to get ripped off, so I asked one of my supervisors to accompany me to a car dealership. We excitedly pulled into the dealership, eyeing which car was going to be my new one. We went through the motions and got to the point at which they ran a credit check. All of this was new to me, so I didn't really understand what was happening. The dealer came back and spoke privately to my supervisor first. I will never forget the look on my supervisor's face. It was one of sheer surprise and distress. I suppose he was trying to figure out how to tell me that my credit was horrendous, and as a result I would be required to pay the highest interest rate known to man.

He eventually did explain this to me, but I had no idea what a credit score or credit report was, let alone what collections accounts were—which apparently were littering my credit report. I explained to him that I had never opened any of those accounts. I was only nineteen years old; this car purchase would be the first credit account I had ever opened. He explained that it was common for youngsters to have accounts opened in their names by family members or identity thieves. Apparently this had happened to me. Throughout my entire childhood, people had been opening accounts in my name—and not paying on those accounts. This identity theft left me in the most abysmal credit position possible. With that type of credit history, I would be lucky if I could even open an account at all.

Although I left that dealership with a new car, it was egregiously expensive. I also left with a new dilemma: I needed to learn everything I could about credit reports and scores so I could repair my own credit. Coincidentally, I had another eye-opening experience involving my credit that same week. My job in the navy required a security clearance, and the background investigation involved conducting credit checks. The security officer summoned me to his office to explain that my negative credit history could lead to the revocation of my security clearance, which would cause me to lose my job! I was mortified! This credit situation was rocking my world! If the dealership experience was not enough to motivate me to repair my credit, then potentially losing my job certainly would be.

I was now on a mission. I contacted any family members I suspected of using my name to open accounts and adamantly told them to cease and desist, because I would be reporting those accounts as fraudulent. I also disputed any account I suspected identity thieves of opening. In addition, I found the best book ever for my situation at the time: *Your Credit Score*, 2nd edition, by Liz Pulliam Weston. I purchased a used copy for under five dollars, and over the next three months I followed her advice to a T. I sent letters, made phone calls, and contacted the credit bureaus to resolve everything. I became obsessed with watching my credit score get better and better. After six months of this, my credit score had increased by 200 points! My credit went from the bottom of the barrel to the cream of the crop.

In the end, I did not lose my navy job, but I was still stuck with that high-interest car loan. However, I wouldn't change that experience for anything. It drove me to learn how to fix and manage my credit, and I have benefited greatly from what I learned to this day. I am in a position to help myself, my relatives, my friends, and my readers repair and manage their credit for a lifetime. This has become very rewarding work for me—financially and emotionally.

Keys to Keeping Good Credit: The keys to maintaining good credit are 1) to always pay your bills on time and in full and 2) to live within your means—not allowing your expenses to exceed your income. In my opinion, it's fine to use a credit card to cover up to 10 percent of your income. This would be primarily to improve your trustworthiness with credit, and to make any small ends meet at the end of a month. For example, if your income is $1000 per month, then $100 per month in expenses can be paid using a credit card. I am adamant about keeping this number low because credit card companies charge interest, and we don't want interest to become a regular expense of yours. Also, the expenses you place on your credit card should be expenses you can easily cut off if you hit a trying financial time—expenses like a gym membership, cable service, etc. You don't want to be stuck incurring interest charges for an expense you can't live without, like rent or car payments.

Keeping a budget and building your savings go hand in hand with keeping a good credit score. If you stick to your budget, you'll end up living within your means and won't have to miss any bill payments. Missing bill payments will drastically lower your score. If you build up your savings, you can dip into them to keep up with your bills if your income is reduced at any time, or if important unexpected expenses arise. Savings can help cover any bill payments until your finances improve.

You will need to regularly check your credit report and score, because credit bureaus commonly make mistakes and identity theft is a real thing. You don't want an erroneous negative account on your report hurting your score. You don't want to have identity thieves using your name and hurting your score without you knowing it. Initially, because I had so much repair work to do, I had a daily monitoring service on my credit reports. After a few years of no credit bureau mistakes or identity theft, I was able to reduce the monitoring to twice a year.

Nowadays, many banks will monitor your score at no cost, which can relieve you of the need to pay for a monitoring service. You will still need to monitor what your bank is reporting to you. If you notice a significant drop in your score, you should actively check all of your reports to ensure that no new negative information is being reported in your name. The point is that your credit report and score are your responsibility. No one will guard them better than you will.

As with budgeting, repairing and maintaining good credit can be tough at first for a beginner. A financial coach will be a good resource to walk through the process with you and give you the tools needed to manage the process on your own.

Buying a Home

After a few years of saving, budgeting, and maintaining at least a 700-level credit score, you may be ready to buy a home! Buying a home can be an exciting time. Your home will likely be your biggest asset, since over time it will most likely increase in value. Sometimes, home values can increase by tens of thousands of dollars or more over the course of five or six years. Your home will also be *all yours*. No more parent or landlord rules, no loud neighbors stomping over your head, and no more rent payments. Much of what you pay toward your home each month will become equity, which means your money will be coming back to you someday.

Buying a home can also be a very stressful time if you don't have a few good tools in your toolbox. Buying a home the abundant way requires having a good credit score and cash—thousands of dollars in cash. You can certainly buy a house without having all of these ducks in a row, but ideally you will start now to build up everything you need to have great home-buying experiences.

We've talked about how to manage your credit score. This is especially important during the home-buying process, because you will be shopping for interest rates, and the best/lowest interest rates go to the customers with the best credit scores. Interest rates matter because a higher rate will cost you much more per month than a lower rate will. One of the first things I did when buying my first home was to read a book on home-buying, and

I focused on the section about interest rates. I would recommend that for you as well.

Having lots of cash during the home-buying process is also a must. There will be plenty of expenses you'll incur during this time that you don't want to have to roll into your mortgage and pay interest for. I'm talking about closing costs—the many small and larger expenses you'll incur during the process of purchasing your home. They can reach up to $20,000 or they can be as low as $5,000. In some cases, you may not incur any closing costs, and you may even incur a *closing credit,* which is money owed to you at the end of the home-buying process.

Your closing costs will be determined by many factors that can't always be precisely predicted. But one factor that will certainly affect them is timing. I've purchased homes in both buyer's and seller's markets, and the costs of home-buying were very different depending on which market it was. Obviously, you will want to try to time your purchase to coincide with a buyer's market, but sometimes it isn't possible to do that. Maybe you just had a child, or went through a divorce, or a had a sudden, sharp increase in rent and you have to find a new home more quickly than you would like to. If you end up having to buy in a seller's market, it is highly likely that you'll incur thousands of dollars in closing costs rather than a closing credit.

I, personally, have never incurred a closing credit. My closing costs were always upwards of $10,000, so I would recommend being financially prepared for such an expense with cash. If you don't have that cash at the end, as mentioned earlier, you will have to pay for those expenses by rolling them into your mortgage, which will cost you thousands of additional dollars' worth of interest. I could never recommend taking a route that will end up costing thousands of dollars in interest. I'd rather recommend a route that encourages you to practice the externals we've discussed and build on those disciplines that you can use for the rest of your life. You should save, budget, and keep a good credit score. These skills will not only benefit you during the home-buying process, but they will provide abundance in every area of your finances.

Paying Taxes

Paying taxes is one of the externals we all must do on a regular basis. I roll my eyes at the thought of them. I don't know anyone who enjoys paying taxes. As you grow in abundance, there will be periods when your income taxes and property taxes will seem to skyrocket. It may feel like you're being robbed! Initially, your natural reaction may be to complain and curse and roll your eyes—but you'll still have to cut that tax check no matter how annoyed you become. For me, it was always painful, and I got tired of feeling the negative energy about it. Besides, the negative energy never changed my tax situations—so I decided I had to change my attitude about it.

I needed a better way to cope with relinquishing tax money, so I searched for spiritual teachings on taxes. Jesus said it best: "Give back to Caesar what is Caesar's." This was His response when asked if He thought it was fair to pay taxes to a corrupt government. I needed to accept the fact that tax money belongs to the government, it doesn't belong to me. Although the money flows into my paycheck, it has to flow out to the government. I chose to use this as a way to practice affirming my value. I resolved that tax money came to me first in order to be touched and blessed by me, then sent off to its proper owner to serve its intended purpose.

This attitude can help you practice a detachment toward tax money, which should relax your energy about it. You'll pay taxes with far less bitterness if you combine a new internal attitude with the external action. That's when I began to see a change, not only in myself but in my tax situation. I was looking for the universe to reward me by reducing my tax obligation. Instead, I was rewarded in a far better way—my income would increase! I was able to afford to pay taxes plus have much more left over! When you are faced with a financial challenge that is eating away at your energy, combine some internal work with the right external action, and the universe will reward you by meeting the need abundantly!

Investing

Investing can be both fun and challenging to explore. It can be invigorating to watch your stocks soar to the sky—but then infuriating to watch them fall to the ground. It's a roller-coaster ride that can be tough to get comfortable with, but you can always start with your 401(k) account. If you aren't an experienced investor, visit your employer's retirement program website and read about all the funds they will be investing your money into. This is a good way to learn some basics about investing while becoming very familiar with your employer's retirement program.

Your retirement account is likely a place where you will

invest decades' worth of income, so I can't think of a better place to start learning. If you don't have a 401(k), then read a For Dummies book on investments and try your hand at the easiest investments first. That's what I did. As you learn, you can start placing your money into more sophisticated investment options—but the point is to hit two birds with one stone by learning about investments and developing your own retirement plan simultaneously.

Investment basics can be written as a book all on its own, so I won't try to delve into every option now. There are so many diverse options on investing, and I would recommend learning that ones that speak to your *being*, based on your tolerance for risk and volatility. For the beginner, researching your 401(k) is a good start. For a novice, reading from your favorite investment authors and/or hiring an investment planner is a good option too. There are many different options for each person's level of skill, but investing is an option that all abundance-minded persons should consider.

There are many advanced financial strategies that you can learn along your journey to abundance, but the basics will never become outdated. They are the foundation of any financial success you'll enjoy in the future. If you haven't been practicing them, start today! Money and time work really well together, and they are eager to work for you. But you have to be the boss and put them to work! Start practicing whichever externals you're most eager to see results from. Connect with your *being* and decide: Are you a hunter ready to invest in the stock market? Are you a steward ready to tweak and twist at a budget to find the best way to maximize your income? Or are you an eagle, protecting and preserving the future with smart saving?

The most important theme of this blueprint is to combine the internal with the external. Everyone says they want wealth—but as the saying goes, "Actions speak louder than words." Yes, you need the basic external actions to get your money moving and working, but you also need the internal actions to keep the money coming back for more. If you use just the basic externals, you'll have basic results. But if you combine the basic externals with the internal work, you'll have abundant results.

"Give back to Caesar what is Caesar's." – Matthew 22:21

CHAPTER 6

In Conclusion:
Be Abundance-Minded

Now you have all the tools you need to start expressing the energy of abundance! You have the internal tools to put your energy into action. You have the external tools to put your money into action. As you move through the blueprint, you should be practicing prudent external actions while maintaining peaceful energy. You've healed some old triggers and you're learning to identify and heal new ones. You don't have to live another five, ten, or fifteen years on the same financial level. You're prepared to go to your next level now.

What You Should Start Doing Now

If you're the person who has mastered the basic external actions but has been missing the blueprint, then your focus should be to start combining your financial skills with good internal energy now. You may have been doing the externals for decades, and now you're enjoying a comfortable financial life—but the key to more abundance is the energy within the blueprint.

There are two new skills I want you to begin practicing

this year: 1) make a mental commitment that whatever financial needs arise this year you will practice the peaceful pattern. Don't allow yourself to wallow in fear for days before you start practicing peace. 2) Add more advanced financial strategies to your arsenal. For example, if you enjoy investing, begin learning new investment skills and strategies. Read a book on an investment strategy that may have intimidated you in the past. The point here is to add one new internal skill and one new external skill to your toolbox this year.

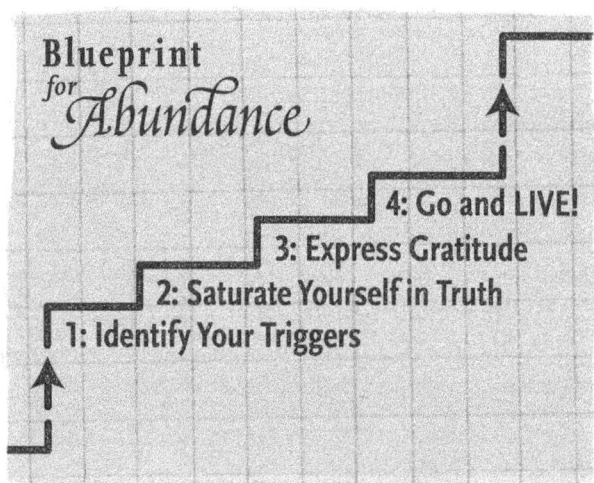

Blueprint *for* **Abundance**

4: Go and LIVE!
3: Express Gratitude
2: Saturate Yourself in Truth
1: Identify Your Triggers

If you're the person who has not been practicing the basic externals, then your focus should be to start practicing them now. The good news is that when you're ready to add in the internal work, you will already have the blueprint available to you. No more just making money and spending it without a better plan. In the beginning, you will need to develop a bit of discipline. You will benefit from a financial coaching program that will take a personalized approach to helping you master the externals. It's a great advantage to have a coach alongside you to help you develop the skills you need more quickly than you would develop them on your own.

There are two new skills I want you to practice this year: 1) commit to paying down any debt you have. My suggestion is to attack smaller debts first then attack your larger debts. For example, if you have a credit card with a $1000 balance and a credit card with a $5000 balance, you should double and triple up payments toward the $1000 card to pay it down first. When you succeed at that, you will have the confidence to attack any other debt you have. 2) Become familiar with your credit reports and scores. As I recommended earlier, *Your Credit Score*, 2nd edition, by Liz Pulliam Weston is a great resource for anyone interested in understanding and improving their credit.

My goal with this book is to shorten the learning curve toward having abundance. If people in their twenties or even their teens could get hold of this blueprint early on, think of the level of abundance they could experience. They could enjoy a lifetime of it without having to struggle so much along the way. That is my dream: that people will enjoy the best things in life without suffering so much to get them.

I want to reignite the fire that convinces people there is abundance all around us. Too many of us are scarcity-minded rather than abundance-minded. We will have what we expect—and the world has not been expecting abundance. The graph on the next page shows the use of the word *abundance* in the English language over time.

For over two hundred years, abundance-mindedness has been in decline! I want more people to be conscious of abundance, to be vocal about abundance, and to experience abundance.

Use over time for: *abundance*

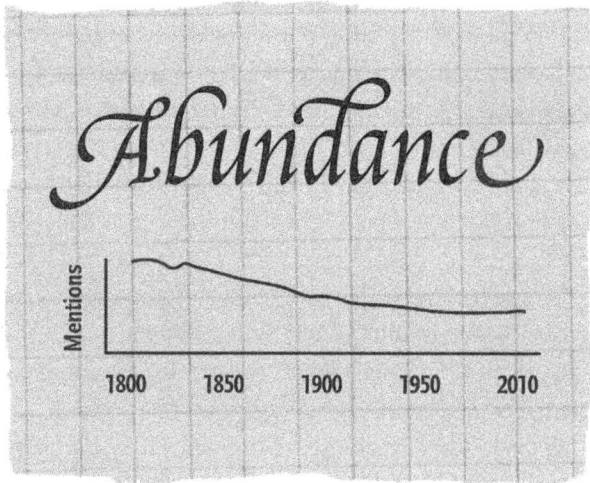

Abundance

Mentions

1800   1850   1900   1950   2010

Why Should You Care?

Why should we care about having abundance—an ample amount of all that we need? Besides the obvious financial gains, we should care because we're here and we get to live a life! Why not take this life as opportunity to have an ample amount of all you need at all times? If all it will take is a little bit of work, why not live life in a way that's wondrous? Most people are just getting up, going to work, and paying bills. That's not a terrible way to live life, but there is not enough magic in that for me. With all that daily life demands from us, it shouldn't be too much to expect abundance. It's not as much about money as it is about life. Money's purpose is to enrich our life experience.

You might say, "What if I try this blueprint and it doesn't work?" I can't guarantee you $1 million if you practice the energy of abundance. But what if you try it and it *does* work? What if you try it and it gets you better connected with yourself, with others, and with the universe? What if you try this and it helps you feel better supported in life, more peaceful, and less stressed? That's what we really want—to feel better in life—and we know money can help us with this. What if this blueprint causes you to be more confident in your ideas and you take more risks to develop them and share them with the world?

What if you give birth to an idea that doesn't produce $1 million right away, but it produces a journey that leads to more than just $1 million? It could be like the book by author Michael Singer, *The Untethered Soul.* Singer wrote his book in 2007, but it wasn't until five years later that it was discovered by Oprah Winfrey, who hailed it as "a beautiful little book." She interviewed Singer about his book in 2012, which you can imagine opened up a whole new world of exposure for him. Once his book was born, its journey took five years before it made it to the right place at the right time.

The more you are convinced that abundance can come easily, the more you will experience it. The energy of abundance is available to people of all ages, all genders, all sexualities, all income levels, all races, all religions— all people. There are no disqualifiers! And there is no completion point. It is something you can enjoy all of your life, because this process is a living model. Although it begins as a linear journey, you will cycle back into it over and over again as life gives you new opportunities for growth.

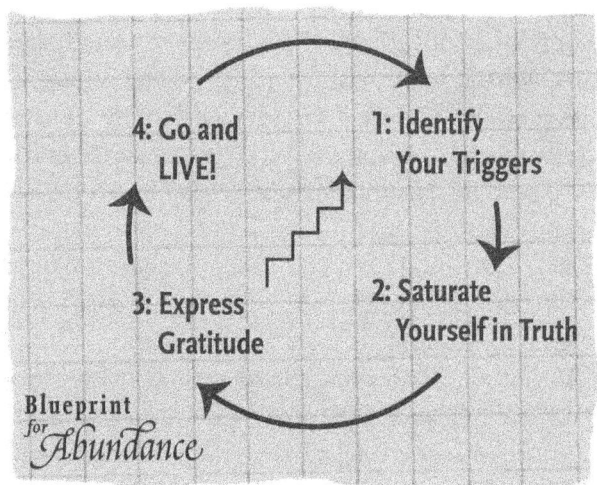

Learning to receive and enjoy abundance is a science and an art; it's technical and magical in ways that can be measured and in ways that are immeasurable. A key part of the word *abundance* is -*dance*, and your journey will be like a dance. When you *watch* a dance, it's beautiful. It flows, it jerks, it jives. But when you *study* a dance, you break it down into every little kick, wave, and jolt. After studying its beauty, you can re-create it. And that's what I want to do with this book. Rather than just experience the benefits of the energy of abundance, I want to understand how it works, and then re-create the beauty for others.

I haven't been sharing any secrets with you. All of this information has been with you—in your soul—that's why you can instinctively connect with it. I've simply served as a messenger, offering a reminder of what you already know. I hope you're able to enjoy the journey of discovering and connecting with yourself and with the universe in a new way. I wish for you not only an abundance of money, but an abundance of everything. Your future matters. Your destiny matters. You deserve to have all the desires of your heart. If you practice resting, healing, saturating yourself in truth, expressing gratitude, and being yourself—an abundance of money will be the least of the riches that will flow to you.

God bless, with love,
Vonnie

Endnotes

1. Getting Started: The Energy of Abundance

people are employing their natural survival instincts: Sheryl Paul, "Health Anxiety, Money Anxiety, and the Fear of Loss: How Our Fear-Based Stories Can Help Us Heal," Thrive Global, September 6, 2018, https://thriveglobal.com/ stories/health-anxiety-money-anxiety-and-the-fear-of-loss/.

2. What Is Abundance?

"Abundance is not something we acquire": Wayne Dyer, quoted in BrainyQuote, accessed April 19, 2019, www.brainyquote.com/quotes/wayne_dyer_154383.

"I had drawn The Color Purple into my life": Oprah Winfrey, interview with Larry King, Larry King Live, first aired May 1, 2007, on CNN, http://transcripts. cnn.com/TRANSCRIPTS/0705/01/lkl.01.html.

introduced the concept of being, doing, and having: Iyanla: Fix My Life, season 5, episode 520, first aired September 29, 2018, on the Oprah Winfrey Network.

her journey to identify more of her being: "Iyanla
Vanzant on Making Peace with Oprah," YouTube, posted
September 9, 2012, by the Oprah Winfrey Network,
https://www.youtube.com/watch?v=jM22oreRPkI.

his competitors referred to him as "a killer": "The
Information Age," episode 6 of *The Nineties*,
first aired August 13, 2017, on CNN.

I recently saw an advertisement: "Talking Money
Is Tough. But It Doesn't Have to Be," advertisement for SoFi, 2018, via Facebook, www.facebook.
com/SoFi/videos/2392680344292856/.

wealthier participants were more likely: Michael
W.Kraus and Dacher Keltner, "Social Class Rank,
Essentialism, and Punitive Judgment," *Journal of
Personality and Social Psychology* 105, no. 2 (August
2013): 247–261, http://dx.doi.org/10.1037/a0032895.

*white-bellied flycatcher monarcha albiventris illus-
trated by elizabeth gould – image: Freepik.com*

3. The Blueprint for Abundance: Triggers

"I'm a king": Derrick Jaxn, "Self-Love: How Do YOU
Practice It?", first aired April 25, 2017, on Facebook Live.

the way to overcome them is to make them conscious:
Eckhart Tolle, *A New Earth: Awakening to Your Life's
Purpose* (New York: Dutton/Penguin Group, 2005).

it would take only five billionaires: "5 Billionaires
Who Could End World Hunger," Borgen
Magazine, June 13, 2014, https://www.borgenmag-
azine.com/5-billionaires-end-world-hunger/.

traditional male dominance in financial matters: Julia
Callegari, Pernilla Liedgren, and Christian Kullberg,
"Gendered Debt—a Scoping Study Review of Research on
Debt Acquisition and Management in Single and Couple
Households," European Journal of Social Work, January
22, 2019, http://dx.doi.org/10.1080/13691457.2019.1567467.

But studies still show: Callegari et al.

One out of every ten: "Americans Are Living Longer,"
USC Leonard Davis School of Gerontology, accessed
April 19, 2019, https://gerontology.usc.edu/resources/
infographics/americans-are-living-longer/.

the reason couples experience increasing pressures: Terri
Orbuch, "Don't Let Money Ruin Your Relationship:
Does Money Cause Tension in Your Relationship?,"
Psychology Today, August 27, 2010, https://www.
psychologytoday.com/us/blog/the-love-doctor/201008/
don-t-let-money-ruin-your-relationship.

open palm image by freepik

4. Express Gratitude and GO LIVE LIFE

"Be thankful for what you have": Oprah Winfrey, quoted in BrainyQuote, accessed April 19, 2019, https://www. brainyquote.com/quotes/oprah_winfrey_163087.

"five ways to express and experience love": Gary Chapman, The Five Love Languages: How to Express Heartfelt Commitment to Your Mate (Chicago: Northfield, 1995).

Words of Affirmation: Chapman.

"When you are grateful": Tony Robbins, quoted in "20 Gratitude Quotes," How to Be Happy, accessed April 19, 2019, https://howtobehappy.guru/gratitude-quotes/.

"Social scientists have found": Chip Conley, quoted in "20 Gratitude Quotes."

"Feeling gratitude and not expressing it": William Arthur Ward, quoted in "20 Gratitude Quotes."

"Gratitude is the healthiest of all human emotions": Zig Ziglar, quoted in BrainyQuote. accessed April 19, 2019, https://www.brainyquote.com/quotes/zig_ziglar_617744.

"Acknowledging the good that you already have": Eckhart Tolle, quoted in "20 Gratitude Quotes."

"Opportunities, relationships, even money flowed my way": Oprah Winfrey, quoted in "20 Gratitude Quotes."

"I don't have to chase extraordinary moments":
Brené Brown, quoted in BrainyQuote, https://www.
brainyquote.com/quotes/brene_brown_553096.

thank you image by rawpixel.com

5. The Externals

In addition, I found the best book: Liz
Pulliam Weston, Your Credit Score, 2nd
Edition (New Jersey: FT Press, 2007)

6. In Conclusion: Be Abundance-Minded

As I recommended earlier: Liz Pulliam Weston, Your
Credit Score, 2nd Edition (New Jersey: FT Press, 2007)

"a beautiful little book": "Michael Singer: Free Yourself
from Negative Thoughts," posted October 4, 2017, by
Oprah's SuperSoul Conversations Podcast, https://
www.youtube.com/watch?v=WbMcUueg4Sc.

About the Author

Vonnie Virgil shows regular people how to generate and maintain financial abundance by coaching them to be sensible, optimistic, and peaceful about money. She has spent years helping those closest to her repair their credit and form better strategies to build their wealth. Now, she is eager to share her strategies with the world. Her dream is to coach people toward having an ample amount of what they need at all times—living in abundance in every way they can.

As a US Navy and Air Force Reserve veteran, she began to discover the need for financial coaching during her service years. Her military colleagues would complain they didn't have time to manage their finances carefully because of their demanding military schedules. She wanted to help with that, so since then she has taken special pride in helping people find the best financial strategies for their personal needs.

Vonnie holds a bachelor's degree in psychology from Northeastern Illinois University and a master's degree in management and leadership from Webster University. She can be reached via Facebook, Twitter, Instagram, email at **vonnievirgil@hotmail.com,** or through her website at **www.vonnievirgil.com.**

www.ingramcontent.com/pod-product-compliance
Lightning Source LLC
Chambersburg PA
CBHW051813040426
42446CB00007B/656